NEW GENETIC ECONOMY
FOUNDER
Taha Bayomy Mohamed

Table of Contents

New Genetic Economy

Introduction

First Chapter: Concept of genetic economy

Historical perspective on economic systems

Definition of the genetic economy of Micro, macro, and global economies with the identification of the type of diseases that affect each of them

Second chapter: How was the founding of the genetic economy?

Using the mathematical approach (The geometric theory) In the establishment of the genetic economy

Third chapter: The geometric genetic economy theory

Firstly: The advantages of geometric theory

Secondly: Important definitions

Thirdly: The geometric genetic economy theory

Fourthly: Summary of the Probabilities of geometric genetic economy theory:

Fourth chapter: The use of geometric genetic economy theory in the foundation of economic models
(Practical study of the model of evaluation of companies)

Firstly: Measure the efficiency of the product of this company

Secondly: Measuring the efficiency of the company's management for general expenses

Thirdly: Measuring the efficiency of the company's management for debit interest

Fourthly: Measuring the efficiency of the company's management in achieving other revenue

Fifthly: measuring the efficiency of those responsible for managing the main activity

Fifth chapter: Practical study of the model of the preparation of the budget

Sixth chapter: Practical study of the model for the preparation of the standard budget

Seventh chapter: Practical study of the model of the credit budget preparation

Eighth chapter: Practical study of the model of the preparation of the budget when the cost of the product rises

Ninth chapter: Practical study of the model of the preparation of the budget when we grant discounts on the selling price

Tenth chapter: The use of geometric genetic economy theory in the foundation of Economic Models of Macroeconomics (Practical study of the model of diagnosis of the sectors of the State)

Eleventh chapter: Practical study of the model of diagnosis of the economic system of the state

Twelfth chapter: The use of geometric genetic economy theory in the foundation of economic models Third: The economic model of the global economy (Practical study of the diagnostic model of companies that are registered on the stock exchange)

Comparing between economic systems:

Questions and exercises at the genetic economy

References

Introduction

Genetic economy is an emerging science that examines the underlying characteristics of economics, where each economic unit has its own distinct characteristics. Through these characteristics, we identify the causes of the disease and thus it can be treated. Therefore, the genetic economy is considered a therapeutic economy for economic problems. This is evident from the definition of the genetic economy, which is as follows:

Definition of the genetic economy:

It is a science that examines the potential characteristics of economics in order to know how this system works (both in the case of health or illness of this system) to identify diseases that affect the economy (at the micro-economic level, the macro economy and the global economy) and to know the reasons which lead to these diseases and how to treat them to ensure the integrity of the work of the economic system from any crises.

Through this book, we will highlight the following points:

How did the genetic economy define microeconomics, macroeconomics, and the global economy?

How did the genetic economy, identify diseases that affect both the micro-economy and the macro-economy and global economy?

A complete study of geometric genetic economy theory and its uses.

Identify the relationship of the genetic economy with economic resources management to maintain it practically, whether economic resources for the micro-economy (at the level of operating companies in the country), macro economy (at the level of sectors of the State or the economic system of the state) or the global economy (at the level of multinational companies) through the economic models that are created by a genetic economy in order to maintain the management of these resources

First Chapter:
Concept of genetic economy

Why the genetic economy

There are many economic systems which the human applied to achieve welfare that the man is looking forward through these systems. However, there are economic crises facing these economic systems, the human being tried to find solutions for these crises. The specialists tried to know the causes of these crises and the solutions to solve these crises. The solution always stops on the extent of the ability of the specialists, their experiences, and their knowledge. Therefore, the results are according to the human element either being right or wrong in determining the problem and subsequently its solution.

So, the genetic economy (it is a therapeutic economy for economic diseases) invents many diagnostic models to detect the economic diseases automatically. Once the case is given to these models, the models give the suitable solution for these diseases without any intervention from the human element that may be right or wrong.

The researcher stayed thirty years to establish this science by using geometric theory to reach the highest degree of accuracy in the results.

The genetic economy can help the reader to become an expert in economics and management, through the models that are created by the genetic economy. These models are as following:

First: Microeconomic level:

Models for diagnosis of the operating companies in the country (either public sector or private sector companies):

Model for diagnosis of the companies

This model aims that the reader acquires practically the following experiences:

How you discover the genes of the company that must comply with the genes of employees of the company (put the fitting man in the right place) and how he knows productivity of these workers and how he knows if this productivity is appropriate with the available resources to the company or not.

How you discover the causes of decreasing of sales, if there is a deficit in financing, quality of the product or the purchasing power of the consumers of the company's product and how to solve that.

How you discover if there is extravagance in general expenses and what are its causes and what are the ways to treat it.

How you discover the negative impact of the loan on the company's activity and how to handle it.

How can you manage the company in the case of economic recession? Moreover, what is the standard that he depended on to invest in the stock market ?

How can you identify the standard that if it is achieved, it is recommended to liquidate the company immediately?

Model of budget preparation

This model aims that the reader acquires practically the following experiences:

How do you use the available resources in order to achieve equivalent profits to these resources taking into account the economic situation that the company works in it?

Model of standard budget preparation

This model aims that the reader acquires practically the following experiences:

How do you use the available resources in order to achieve equivalent profits to these resources taking into account the economic situation that the company works in it?

How do you know the responsible for non-implementation of the company's budget marketing manager or general manager?

Model of credit budget preparation

This model aims that the reader acquires practically the following experiences:

You will know the factor that makes him to recommend borrowing or not from the bank.

Model of budget preparation when costs increased

This model aims that the reader acquires practically the following experiences:

You will know the factor that achieves the interests of the company and to be good competitor in the market when the cost of the product is rising.

Model of budget preparation when the company grants discount on the sale price

This model aims that the reader acquires practically the following experiences:

You will know the factor that achieves the interests of the company and be good competitor in the market when the company grants discount on the sale price.

All previous models that mentioned in the genetic economy aimed at the end that the reader should be an economic consultant to all companies, able to determine the stumbled companies, work to treat those companies and to identify the pioneer companies in order to benefit from them to increase the state revenues, and thus we preserve the country's economic fortunes.

Second: **Macroeconomics level**:

Model for diagnosis of state sectors:

This model aims that the reader acquires practically the following experiences :

When it is recommended to increase, stabilize or support production inputs for the evaluated sector and when to stop importing similar goods.

When it is recommended to stabilize or reduce of the exchange rate and debit interest rate.

When it is recommended to impose a progressive tax to control prices.

When it is recommended to hold international agreements to market the products of this sector and when to attract investment for this sector .

This model aims to detect how to use financial, monetary, and legislative policies to control markets, give support, activate the market in this sector and attract the investment for the operating companies in this sector.

Model for diagnosis of economic system of the country :

This model aims that the reader acquires practically the following experiences :

This model aims to detect the purchasing power that shows the equitable distribution of wealth to members of society .

Note: Genetic economy achieves massive revenues for the state without the companies or the citizens bears the burden.

The diagnostic model of the sectors of the state and the diagnostic model of the economic system of the state that mentioned in the macro economy aim that the reader will be an economic consultant to both ministers in terms of determining how to use financial, monetary and legislative policy and to the Prime Minister in terms of how to achieve social justice.

Third: global Economy level:

Model of the diagnosis of stock companies in the world

This model aims that the reader acquires practically the following experiences :

How to recognize the standard to depend on it to invest in the stock market or not.

Note: The genetic economy also establishes the biggest economic database by which the GATT is achieved.

The model of diagnosis of stock companies in the world, which is mentioned in the global economy aims that the reader will be an economic consultant to multinational companies.

Historical perspective on economic systems

Economic systems have passed through several stages; we briefly mention these systems as follows:

Individual economy system:

We used the system verbal to express that a person takes its administrative decision to meet their basic needs through the environment, which he was inhabited, and this was at the beginning of human existence on earth.

The primitive economic system:

In this system, the tribe or clan takes its decision based on what agreed upon them to meet different needs. The products or output wealth will be distributed evenly to the members of the tribe or clan.

An economic system based on the idea of feudalism:

In this system appeared the importance of the first element of the production elements, namely earth, where the ground is considered a source of wealth and the feudal takes its administrative decision in order to increase his fortune by an agriculture maximum space.

An economic system based on the idea of industrial crafts:

In this system appeared the importance of the second element of the production elements, namely labor, where the life has evolved, and slaves began to escape from agriculture at feudal and learned a new craft. This craft has a chairman (representative of the corporation in modern times) who has administrative decision, which regulates the work of artisans.

Capitalist economic system:

This system passed through several stages which had an influence on the thinking of the founders of this system. Among them geographical discoveries stage and discovering many places that has different fortunes, which led to increase the knowledge about the geography of the world and its inhabitants. Thus, it increased the wealth of the discoverers, which transferred to the second phase. The second phase is trading with the new world's population, taking advantage of the scientific and economic backwardness which increased the wealth of these traders. Then capitalist thought moved to the third stage. The stage of the Industrial Revolution where the third element, namely capital appeared. The capitalist makes use of the production elements (land, labor, capital, and management) to increase their wealth, even if they used the fourth phase, a phase of colonialism where the owner of the money took the administrative decision. Taking advantage of both the workers, the land and the machine (which appeared in the Industrial Revolution) for the production of low-cost goods and services and sold by the most expensive prices in the colonies to maximize the wealth of the owners of capital.

From the above the capitalist economic system characterizes that individuals possessed the production elements (land – labor - capital - Management) and thus they possess the returns under the slogan (let he works - let he passes) and that the markets are organized under the principle of (supply and demand),

This system falls in the following errors:

Achieving special interests for the category of capitalist, apart to achieve the social justice for the rest of society Categories.

The concentration of wealth in a few hands in the community with depriving a wide range from this wealth.

There is a large segment of society is suffering from the weakness of purchasing power that meets his needs.

Self-sufficiency is not achieved, but in the rare case when there are savings of natural resources as well as the technological wealth output in the country.

In the capitalist economic system invests in profitable sectors rather than other sectors even if the other sectors are strategic sectors in the state, which leads to an imbalance in the implementation of the economic plan.

Result of the misguided policies that practiced in capitalist systems, which leads to congestion of the laboring classes against category of the capitalist. This leads to a lack of security and stability of the country and this is what rich countries avoided by granting subsidies for the laboring classes.

Socialist economic system:

The socialist economic system appeared as the result of the exploitation of the capitalist economic system to a class of workers, it named (the exploitation of man to his brother) and for the treatment of this exploitation, the ownership of the production elements (land - labor - capital - administration) transported from individuals to the State where State manages those elements. The administrative decision is central and in the hands of the state only as it plans, produces, monitors, and distributes the output according to the efforts of the community members of work and effort in order to achieve social justice.

This system also falls in the following errors:

Mismanagement, this is due to that Socialist economic system has not any definitive evaluation tool to put the right man in the right place. As well as the lack of tool define us our mistakes, which occurred in the economic system (both at the micro level or macro-economic)

Wasting of natural resources, as well as weakness of the output of technological innovations because of the weakness of the incentive to produce such innovations.

Increase the volume of expenses than the volume of the revenues, which led to the state borrowing.

The existence of unproductive disguised unemployment.

This economy worked against the instinct of humanity in terms of his love to own, which led to the moral imbalance in terms of bribery and the use of the power badly.

Definition of the genetic economy of Micro, macro, and global economies with the identification of the type of diseases that affect each of them

There are multiple diseases, according to the economic level of the economic system as follows:

At the micro-economic level (companies)

There is not a precise definition of micro-economic that leads us to determine the economic problems facing this economy. Where definitions came distorting. It mentions sometimes that the micro-economic expressed about consumer behavior. Moreover, sometimes about supply and demand and the saying "let him work, let him pass" and therefore the current economic systems are not able to determine the diseases that stem from microeconomics.

Definition of micro-economics :

The genetic economy defined the micro-economics that: it is all economic units (companies and corporations irrespective of their legal form) which both the human capital (who are all workers in this economic unit ranging from senior management and executive departments) and physical capital (capital - Machines - land - innovations etc....) synergize together. Human capital and physical capital express the economic inputs in order to produce a product (whether the product was goods or service). This product has added value and express about economic output, which returns revenue to economic units and works on its continuation through desire of the others to pay the equivalent of this product in order to satisfy human desires.

From the above definition we can identify diseases that arise from the microeconomic (at the companies' level). There are four diseases as follows:

The first disease:

This disease relates with human element and their works, and how to measure their productivity with the efficiency of working capital return and the available resources to the company.

The second disease:

This disease is related to efficiency of the company's management to manage the available resources to the companies in order to achieve the equivalent rate to exploit it.

The third disease:

This disease is related to specifications and quality that is required in the products of these companies for marketing.

The fourth disease:

This disease is related to how to deal with purchasing power to company's customers.

Where it must find a diagnostic tool in order to detect any disease from four diseases that hit the company and therefore its impact on the infrastructure of the economy (microeconomic)

At the macroeconomic level (sectors of the state - and the state itself)

Definition of macroeconomics:

Genetic economy defines the macroeconomic as: it is the state's ability to manage all sectors in microeconomic system (industrial, agricultural, commercial and service) through financial, monetary and regulatory policy tools to reach the self-sufficiency from the products and provide what is missing through the importation after these sectors provide needed currency through export surpluses of some local products (the balance of commercial and service from the balance of payments). The goal of the state of microeconomics system management is getting better revenues (taxes - customs - duties ... etc.) to be added to other sovereign revenues of the state. This income is used to achieve the general objectives of the state that it wants to implement (such as a personal of state - infrastructure - the achievement of social justice as education and health services and subsidies, etc.)

From the above definition, we can identify diseases that arise from a macroeconomic there are four diseases as follows:

The first disease:

Lack of self-sufficiency of goods and services.

The second disease:

Weakness of the export capacity to provide hard currency.

The third disease:

The inability to attract investment (which is what we will discuss in the definition of the global economy).

The Fourth disease:

Weakness of state revenues and therefore government spending in order to achieve social justice and provide goods and services represented in the education, health, scientific research, and eliminating the unemployment and poverty and national security... etc.

They treated the economic problems that facing the macro-economy by economic specialists according to their knowledge and experience without the use of diagnostic model that determines the type of problem and therefore the type of treatment for the problem. Without human intervention, which may be right or wrong, and this is due to the lack of economic database that should be available in each country. Where according to this database that must use the diagnostic models to determine the economic problem and determine how to treat them. The diagnostic models are useful to identify the pioneer companies, which enable the state to double its revenues in order to increase government spending to achieve social justice for members of the community alike.

At the level of the global economy (multinational companies)

Definition of the global economy: Genetic economy defines the global economy as "it is the ability, extent of movement of the global capital across the borders of different countries for the development of these funds benefiting from relative advantages which are provided by the state that wants those funds. These features may be available naturally in the state where the capital is invested, or these features arise through international conventions and at the same time the host country achieves their goals that aspire to achieve from these funds

Note: The global economic system does not mean freedom of global trade in goods and services between countries as it is found in the balance of commercial and service from balance of payments and is located in the macroeconomic). But the global economic system is intended, as I pointed out the freedom of capital movement itself (funds - machines - technological innovations ... etc.), leading to change of the economic shape of the state in terms of the quality of products and the degree of their growth.

From the above definition, we can identify diseases that arise from the global economy and diseases are as follows:

The first disease:

A disease resulting from the lack of global capital movement.

The second disease:

A disease resulting from the failure to achieve the goal of moving global capital.

The two diseases were treated by the ability of politicians to negotiate with foreign investment entities (whether states or multinational companies) without relying on a database identifies the pioneer companies to the leading investors in the host country to this money and in any areas invest.

Second chapter:
How was the founding of the genetic economy?

Firstly: Identifying the economic genes and the relation of the disease of these genes to the micro, macro, and the global economy

Collection of the available data and information about the problem

By reference to the definition of micro-economy, we find that the economic unit contains the following elements:

The first element:

Produce a product (whether this product is a goods or service).

The second element:

Combination of human capital (workers and staff and what they earn from wages and salaries) with the Physical capital (the product share of current expenses and its share of the investment costs).

The third element:

This product has been added -value to work on the continuation of the economic unit - (case of profit or loss in the result)

From the previous three elements, we can identify these cells.

The first cell (first gene):

The Product (which is the first element) and has the following

The first characteristic:

The product has a sale price - and this from economic output

The second characteristic:

The product has costs to be outfitted - and this from economic input.

The third characteristic:

The product has a result (gross profit, loss, or equality) when we subtract the product costs from the sale price

Therefore, it necessitated the student to study the following sciences to figure out the previous three features, by which the product is characterized

Production Management (to know if the production is continuous - by request - Constructions ... etc.).

Cost Accounting (to know if the product bears full direct and indirect costs).

Principles of Marketing (to know product pricing and how to market).

Financial Accounting (To find out how to access to determine the added value from profit or loss).

Individual management.

Studies in the Behavioral Sciences.

Disease, which affects cell of the product and how to treat it

At the microeconomic level

To know if the human element is compatible with the work that was done and how to measure their productivity by comparing with an efficiency of working capital turnover and available economic resources to the Company (i.e. put the right man in the right place)

The treatment of this disease, we will identify it through companies' diagnosis and evaluation model

At the macroeconomic level

Determine the ability of this product to bear the productivity and customs fees (Financial policy) as well as the ability of this product to bear the bank interest and prevailing exchange rates (monetary policy) as well as the extent of this product need to stop the importation of similar goods (legislative policy). Or vice versa this product requires support from the state.

This necessitated studying the follows:

General Financial Economics (to learn the required financial and monetary policy)

Foreign Trade Theory (to learn the customs legislation between states).

Treating these diseases depends on the efficiency that achieved with this product (We will learn about it through the use of geometric theory in the diagnosis and evaluation model for companies and sectors of the state).

The second cell (second gene):

General and administrative expenses and this is from economic input

We pointed out at the second element that the product of economic unit incurs other expenses than the cost of its production, represented in the form of salaries and administrative expenses in addition to its share of investment costs (depreciation). All of this is called general and administrative expenses and have the following features:

The first characteristic:

Gross profit is before general and administrative expenses (when we subtract the product costs from the sale price).

The second characteristic:

The general administrative expenses are from the burdens - that is becoming one of the economic inputs.

The third characteristic:

There is result from general and administrative expenses, which represented in the net profit, loss, or equality (when we subtract general and administrative expenses from the gross profit).

So necessitated the student to study the following sciences with the above to know the previous three features that the general and administrative expenses characterized.

Financial Management and Planning (to know all the aspects that enter financial planning, including the general expenses)

Administrative accounting (to learn how to rationalize the decision in general expenses management).

Labor law (to see the minimum and maximum to prevailing salaries and wages in the state).

Diseases, which affect cell of general and administrative expenses and how to treat them

At the microeconomic level

To know if there is extravagance in general and administrative expenses or not) all this preserves the available economic resources for the economic unit).

The treatment of this disease will be via the diagnostic model, which give us automatically estimated budget that must be implemented to maintain the economic resources.

The third cell (third gene):

Debit interest and this is from economic input

Some economic units may need to use one of economic resources (bank loans) in order to run economic Unit works. Therefore, the economic unit bears burden of paying debit interest to banks in return for the loan. The debit interest has the following attributes:

The first characteristic:

Net profit is before debit interest (when we subtract the general administrative expenses from gross profit).

The second characteristic:

The debit interest is from the burdens - that is becoming one of the economic inputs.

The third characteristic:

There is result to debit interest, which is the net profit, loss or equality (when we subtract debit interest from the net profit that concern to general administrative expenses).

So necessitated the student to study the following sciences with the above in order to know the previous three features that the debit interest characterized.

The financing (To learn how to complete the loan process and funding for economic units).

monetary and banks (as one of the available economic resources of the Economic Unit).

Specialized Accounting (and which is defined by corporations which lend the economic units).

Diseases, which affect debit interest cell and how to treat them

At the microeconomic level

To know the impact of debit interest negatively on the results of the economic unit or not.

The treatment of this disease by diagnostic model, which give us credit budget that determines the excess sales in order to be sold to cover the debit interest .

At the macroeconomic level

To know the effect of the prevailing debit interest rate in the state on the results of economic units and therefore we can decide to raise or lower the debit interest rate .

The fourth cell (fourth gene):

Other revenues and this are from economic output

Sometimes some of the economic units invest part of its economic resources in the outside activity (especially in the case of economic recession) to achieve the so-called other revenue and this improves the results of economic unit. Moreover, other revenues have the following attributes:

The first characteristic:

Net profit is before other revenues (when we subtract the debit interest from the net profit, equality or loss that concern to general administrative expenses result) .

The second characteristic:

The other revenues are becoming one of the economic outputs .

The third characteristic:

There is a result to other revenues, which is the net profit, loss, or equality (when we add other revenues to the net profit, equality or loss that concern to debit interest).

The Fifth cell (Fifth gene):

Efficiency of the responsible for the management of the main activity

Any economic unit characterized that it has economic sources (sources are in the paid-up capital and what achieved from profits and reserves) in addition to the financing sources of loans and other sources like the facilities that obtained by the economic unit from others. These economic resources used in getting all current, fixed and investment assets in order to operate its activity. As a result of the practice of economic unit to its activity, it will achieve either profit, loss or equality. We will know the efficiency of the responsible for the management of the main activity by rewarding those profits to the available sources of economic unity, so the efficiency of responsible for the management of the main activity has these features:

The first characteristic:

Value of available assets in the economic unit (value of current assets + value of fixed assets + value of investment assets) and that is from economic output

The second characteristic:

The value of available sources in the economic unit (equity capital value before adding the profit / loss for the same year that is achieved by the economic unit + the value of the facilities obtained from others) and this is from economic input .

The third characteristic:

The value of profits made by the economic unit of the same year (which is the value of sales minus the value of the cost of sales and the value of general expenses only).

So necessitated the student to study the following to find out the previous three features:

Performance evaluation indicators (to learn how to evaluate the performance of responsible for the management of main activity)

Operations Research in Management (to learn the best ways that should be taken in managing)

Feasibility studies (to learn the feasibility of continuing the project and the extent of achievement of the desired goals)

Diseases, which affect the efficiency of the responsible for the management of the main activity cell and how to treat them

At the microeconomic level

Through this cell, we will know the pioneer companies and troubled companies, where the troubled companies infected with one of the following diseases or all of them :

Weakness of efficiency of the responsible for the management of the main activity in the economic unit (human element).

The existence of a physical problem leads to malfunctioning the production (physical element).

The existence of deficiencies in the quality of the product.

The existence of weak purchasing power for consumers

Note: The treatment of these diseases will be via the diagnostic model, which budget comes out automatically in order to determine the equivalent profit to the available sources in the economic unit.

At the macroeconomic level ,

Where efficiency of the responsible for the management of the main activity from:

To know if the sector needs to market and promote its products internally or externally or no.

To know if the sector needs to be supported or no.

To know if the sector needs to apply progressive taxation in order to reduce the high price or no.

The sixth cell (sixth gene):

Efficiency of the responsible for the management of the main activity and value of loans

It is the same efficiency of the responsible for the management of the main activity in addition to other economic sources like the value of loans which the economic unit borrowed from others and carried the burden of payment the debit interest value. Therefore, the efficiency of the responsible for the management of the main activity in addition to the value of the loans has the following attributes :

The first characteristic:

Value of available assets in the economic unit (value of current assets + value of fixed assets + value of investment assets) and that is from economic output.

The second characteristic:

The value of available sources in the economic unit (equity capital value before adding the profit / loss for the same year that is achieved by the economic unit + the value of the facilities obtained from others + the value of loans) and this is from economic input .

The third characteristic:

The value of profits made by the economic unit for the same year (which is the value of sales minus the value of the cost of sales and the value of general expenses and debit interest).

Diseases, which affect the efficiency of the responsible for the management of the main activity and value of loans cell and how to treat them

At the microeconomic level

Through this cell, we will know the pioneer companies and troubled companies where troubled companies are infected with one of the following diseases or all of them:

Weakness of efficiency of the responsible for the management of the main activity in the economic unit (human element).

The existence of a physical problem leads to malfunctioning the production (physical component).

The existence of deficiencies in the quality of the product.

The existence of weakness in purchasing power for consumers.

Note: The treatment of these diseases will be via the diagnostic model, by which budget comes out automatically that should be implemented in order to determine the equivalent profit to the available sources for the economic unit.

At the macroeconomic level

The efficiency of the responsible for the management of the main activity and value of loans will tell us the following:

If the sector needs to market and promote its products internally or externally or not.

If the sector needs to be supported or not.

If the sector needs to put progressive taxation in order to reduce the high price or not.

If this sector is attractive for investment or not.

The seventh cell (seventh gene):

The efficiency of the responsible for the management of the main activity, the value of loans and facilities that the economic unit took without any cost.

It is the same efficiency of the responsible for the management of the main activity in addition to other economic sources like the value of loans which has cost (debit interest) and facilities value that the economic unit took from another without cost. Therefore, the efficiency of the responsible for the management of the main activity in addition to the value of the loans and facilities that the economic unit took at no cost have the following attributes :

The first characteristic:

Value of available assets for the economic unit (value of current assets + value of fixed assets + value of investment assets) and that is from economic output.

The second characteristic:

The value of available sources for the economic unit (The value of property rights before adding the profit / loss for the same year that is achieved by the economic unit + the value of the facilities obtained from others + the value of loans) and this is from economic input.

The third characteristic:

The value of profits made by the economic unit for the same year (which is the value of sales minus the value of the cost of sales, the value of general expenses, debit interest and other revenues).

Diseases, which affect the cell of efficiency of the responsible for the management of the main activity, the value of loans and facilities that the economic unit took without cost

At the microeconomic level

Here we will know how economic unit mangers act in the economic recession. Did they invest part of their economic resources to achieve other revenues or no to improve the results of the economic unit ?

Using the mathematical approach (The geometric theory) In the establishment of the genetic economy

Notes:

We learned about the environment which the economic diseases arise which they are microeconomic science (economic units), as well as macroeconomic science (public finance economics, financial and monetary policies and legislation).

We identified the cells (seven genes) which are infected with these diseases and how to treat them, where these genes were classified into:

The economic inputs

The economic output

The economic result (from profit, loss, or equality)

And now we must find the answer to these two questions which will help us in building diagnostic models, namely:

The first question:

What is the mechanism that enables us to detect the disease?

Second question:

How to determine the type of disease?

To answer the first question: what is the mechanism that enables us to detect the disease?

The researcher studied all the mathematical sciences (Science of differentiation and integration - Statistics - algebra - geometric sciences ... etc.) he found that the best mechanism used to enable us to detect the disease is the geometric theory, why?

What is the difference between the value of algebra and the value of geometric ?

To illustrate this, we will put the following examples:

In the triangle A B C where the ribs were as follows:

A B = 5 cm   AC = 3 cm   BC = 4 cm

When we talk about algebraic value to rib AB, which is equal to 5 cm it means that the length of the rib of AB = 1 cm (unit of measurement) + 1 cm + 1 cm + 1 cm + 1 cm = 5 cm

When we talk about the geometric value to the rib AB which is equal to 5 cm and its relationship to other two ribs (AC = 3 cm and BC = 4 cm), we find that the rib AB, which holds the algebraic value (which is 5 cm) this rib becomes have a new significance (after it was named rib) so have another name the Hypotenuse, because it is in front of right angle and due to rib AC = 3 cm and rib BC = 4 cm

Therefore, the geometric theory gives significance to the value of algebraic that benefits us in the characterization of the event (in this case, that this is a right-angled triangle) .

Another example (which is derived from the theory of geometric genetic economy)

If the economic unit achieved losses (- 4 $) per sold unit at evaluation standard equal zero. The required is to reach for the sale price, as well as the cost of this unit.

When we talk about the value of algebra, we will find these possibilities (addition, subtraction, multiplication or division) and these possibilities are as follows:

When we talk about the value of algebra, we will find these possibilities (addition or subtraction, multiplication or division) and these possibilities are as following:

The first possibility, the addition = -4 + Zero = -4

The second possibility, the subtraction = -4 - zero = -4

The third possibility, the multiplication = -4 x zero = zero

The fourth possibility, the division = -4 /zero = this value is undefined (it is infinity)

Did we reach the sale price or the cost of the unit? Of course, no.

When we talk about the geometric value of this example, we will use the following geometric equation:

The cost of the unit = (profit or loss of the unit * evaluation standard) - (profit or loss of the unit) * 2

(-4 * zero) - (-4 *2)=

Zero +8= 8

The sale price of this unit = the cost of the unit + (profit or loss of this unit)

8- 4=4

We reached that the sale price = 4$

And the unit cost = 8$

And the loss of the unit = -4 $

All that when the evaluation standard is equal to zero

Here, we can see the significance of evaluation standard, When we use a zero value to the evaluation standard in algebra equation, we did not come up with anything, but when we used the zero value to the evaluation standard in the geometric equation, we came up to the value of sale price and the cost of the unit because the value of zero to evaluation standard have a significant, that the sale price of the unit is half the value of the cost, causing losses for the sold unit.

So, if it is mentioned that the evaluation standard is zero (alone), that indicates that the economic unit achieved revenue is half the cost value which leads to losses without the knowledge of other values (the value of sale price - the value of cost of unit - and the value of the losses that have been made) and this is the scientific miracles to use geometric theories. Therefore, the researcher stayed thirty years to achieve such results.

Answer of the second question: How to determine the type of the disease?

Previously we mentioned that any economic unit carrying seven genes and these genes might get sick, how can we discover the diseases of these genes?

To illustrate this, we put the following example:

If the standard of product gene is 3 (for example) This indicates that this product achieves the big gross profit.

If the standard of the general expense gene is zero (for example), This indicates that general expenses achieved losses that made the cost is twice the revenue.

Then, we judge the general expenses' gene that there is extravagance in these expenses (there is waste in economic resources) because it made the standard of the product, (which was equal to 3) fall in the standard of zero when we used the general expenses. This indicates to disease of general expenses gene and not a product gene disease.

The last question is how to treat the disease that appears

From advantages of using geometric theories, that geometric theory has logic and conclusions as the geometric theory has the ability to reach the proof (in our case is the evaluation standard) when we provide the data (in our case sale price and cost of the unit for example) and vice versa. This is another advantage in using geometric theory, if we gave the previous proof as given data (in this case it would be the evaluation standard) we will get new required desired results (in this case, the value of the sale price and the cost of the unit).

Explanatory example

If evaluation standard for general expenses is zero, which indicates the achievement of losses, so we can use new evaluation standard is 5 (for example, which indicates to the profitability) instead of the standard which is equal to zero. The new evaluation standard will give us the adjusted values for sale price and cost of the unit and general expenses (it is rationalization of general expenditures) where the sale price will achieve profits because the evaluation standard which is equal to 5 indicates to the profitability of the economic unit.

Note: Using (the seven genes), which represent the elements of the geometric theory (the value of the economic input, the value of economic output and economic results) the diagnostic models will be built to identify the type of disease and thus these models of diagnostic will treat these diseases

Third chapter:
The geometric genetic economy theory
Firstly: The advantages of geometric theory

The geometric theory has logic and conclusions.

If the data is given to the geometric theory, it will give you the proof (this proof has indicated where we can use this indication in the diagnosis of any situation and the discovery of the disease). And vice versa if you give to the geometric theory the proof it will give you the previous data (in this case we can use the new data to treat the situation with the use of a better indication of what has been achieved).

There is no doubt about the infrastructure of geometric theory and therefore no questioning about the results.

The geometric theory must be valid for practical application (which is what enables us to confirm the results of hypotheses).

Secondly: Important definitions

Definition of economic inputs:

It is human effort output to use physical component, whether monetary capital, natural resources, technological Innovations within the limits of current expenditures and the share of these inputs from capital expenditures (called economic input by several names, among them the cost of sales or purchases and the economic inputs valued by monetary value of the state).

Definition of economic outputs:

It is the value of economic input that include added value after these outputs are suitable for uses that targeted to be achieved (called economic output, the value of sales and the economic outputs valued by the monetary value of the state).

Definition of economic result:

It is the added value. The result will be achieved when we subtract the value of economic inputs (cost of sales) from the value of economic output (sales) which has three chances either profit, loss, or equality.

Economic evaluation standard:

The economic evaluation standard is a measuring tool for economic input, output and added value. If economic evaluation standard mentioned alone, it would indicate the presence of the economic problem or not.

Available sources of the company

It is all what possessed by the economic unit (the company) from fixed, current assets, or investments, whether the company possessed by its capital or by facilities or credit from others

Thirdly: The geometric genetic economy theory

We knew previously the economic diseases that infect the seven genes. Therefore, we classified these genes into the following three elements:

The first element: The economic input

The second element: The economic output

The third element: The economic results

From (1- profit 2- or equality 3- or loss)

We will add a fourth element, called the evaluation standard, which his task is to measure the performance of each of the economic input and output as well as the economic results and to know the economic performance of the economic systems

From the previous four elements, the elements of the geometric triangle which concerns geometric genetic economy theory will be completed, which are as following:

The geometric genetic economy theory is summarized in the following form:

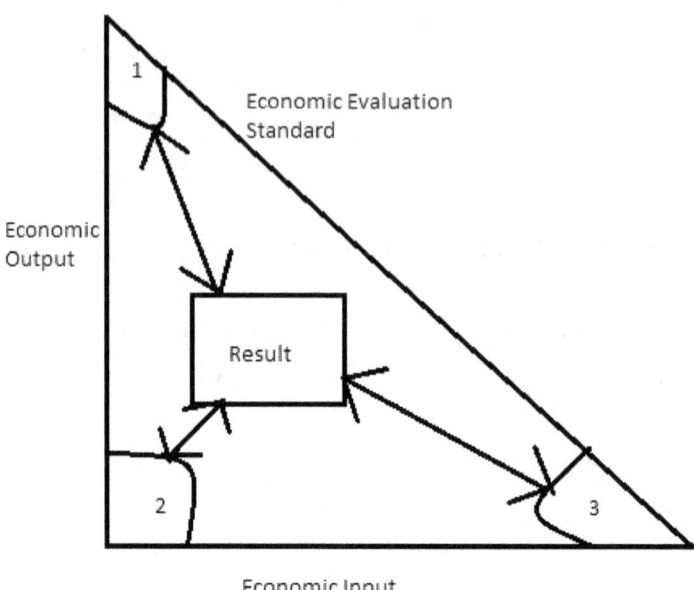

Logic of geometric genetic economy theory

The economic evaluation standard is a tool to measure the work of the economic system

(And this is due to if the economic evaluation standard is mentioned alone, it indicates the success of the economic system or not)

The first conclusion of the theory

If you give the value of two ribs in the previous triangle, the theory will give you the value of the third rib and the angle, which indicates on the result of the work of the economic system (as a proof).

Probabilities of the first conclusion to the theory

First Probability of the first conclusion of the theory

If the economic output value and economic input value are given to the theory as data (first rib and second rib), The theory will give you the economic evaluation standard (third rib) and the value of a result of the economic system (which is one of Triangle angles) as proof.

The following is, the equations that are used to extract the economic evaluation standard and the economic resultant. They are as the following:

The first case:

When the economic unit achieves profit

Example:

If the value of sales (which is from economic output) = 900$

If the value of the cost of sales (which is from economic input) = 800$

The required:

Economic resultant (the value of net profit).

The economic evaluation standard.

The solution:

Economic resultant (profit) = the value of sales - value of sales cost = 900 - 800 = 100

Economic evaluation standard= (sales value - value of sales cost * 0.5)) / economic resultant (profit)

= (900 - (800 * 0.5)) / 100 = 5

The second case:

When an economic unit achieves equality (There is no profit or loss)

Example:

If the value of sales (which is from economic output) = 800$

If the value of the sales cost (which is from economic input) = 800$

The required:

Economic resultant (the value of equality).

The economic evaluation standard.

The solution:

Economic resultant (equality) = the value of sales - value of sales cost = 800 – 800 = zero

Economic evaluation standard = (sales value - value of sales cost * 0.5)) /economic resultant (equality)

=(800 - (800 * 0.5)) / zero = undefined value (infinity)

The third case:

When an economic unit achieves losses. The value of sales is less than the total value of the sale cost and more than half the value of the sale cost.

Example:

If the value of sales (which is from economic output) = 700$

If the value of sales cost (which is from economic input) = 800$

The required:

Economic resultant (the value of losses).

The economic evaluation standard.

The solution:

Economic resultant (losses) = the value of sales - value of sales cost = 700 - 800 = -100

Economic evaluation standard = (sales value - value of sales cost * 0.5) / economic resultant (losses)

= (700 - (800 * 0.5)) / -100 = -3

The fourth case:

When an economic unit achieves losses, (i.e. the value of sales is equal to half the value of the sales cost)

Example:

If the value of sales (which is from economic output) = 400$

If the value of the sales cost (which is from economic input) = 800 $

The required:

Economic resultant (the value of losses).

The economic evaluation standard.

The solution:

Economic resultant (losses) = the value of sales - value of sales cost = 400 – 800 = -400

Economic evaluation standard = (sales value – (value of sales cost) * 0.5) / economic resultant (losses)

= (400 - (800 *0.5)) / - 400 = zero

The fifth case:

When an economic unit achieves losses, the value of sales is less than half the value of the sales cost.

Example:

If the value of sales (which is from economic output) = 300$

If the value of the sales cost (which is from economic input) = 800

The required:

Economic resultant (the value of losses).

The economic evaluation standard.

The solution:

Economic resultant (losses) = the value of sales - value of sales cost = 300 – 800 = -500

Economic evaluation standard = (sales value - value of sales cost * 0.5)) /economic resultant (losses)

= (300 - (800 * 0.5)) / -500 = 0.2

Note: This possibility with its five cases will be used in the economic evaluation of the five cases, the indications of the economic evaluation standard can be summarized in the form of the following table:

The outputs of genetic economy theory (indications of economic evaluation standard)

The degrees of economic efficiency are determined according to the following

The case of the profit

In this case, the degrees of economic evaluation standards are integer and positive numbers or integer and positive numbers including fractions. The degrees of economic evaluation standard are divided into

From 1 to 2 degrees, it expresses an excellent degree of profit

From 2.01 to 4 degrees, it expresses a very good degree of profit

From 4.01 to 7 degrees, it expresses a good degree of profit

From 7.01 to 12 degrees, it expresses an acceptable degree of profit

From 12.01 up to 50 degrees, it expresses a weak degree of profit

From 50.01 up to infinity degree, it expresses a very weak degree of profit

The case of equality

In this case, the degree of the evaluation standard is equal to undefined value (infinity)

The case of losses

when revenue is greater than the average cost and less than the total cost)

In this case, the degrees of economic evaluation standard are integer and negative numbers or integer and negative numbers including fractions

The case of losses

when revenues are equal to the average total cost

In this case, the degree of economic evaluation standard is equal to zero

The case of losses

when revenue is less than the average cost

In this case, the degree of economic evaluation standard is only positive fraction numbers

Very important note:

From the above table if we mentioned the value of the Evaluation standard alone, it indicated the success of the economic unit, whether it achieved profit, loss or equality, and this is the main objective of the use of geometric theory

Second possibility of the first conclusion of the theory

If the economic output value and the value of the economic evaluation standard are given to the theory as data (first rib and third rib), the theory will give you value of the economic inputs (second rib) and the result of the economic system (which is one of the angles of a triangle) as proof.

The following equations are used to extract the value of economic resultant and economic inputs, they are as following:

Here we will use the first case that is the profit. The reader can use the same equations with the other four cases:

Case of equality .

The case of losses when the revenue is less than the value of the total costs and more than half the value of costs.

The case of losses when the revenue is equal to half the value of costs

The case of loss when revenue is less than half the cost value

By choosing the evaluation standard value as shown in table (indications of economic evaluation standard) page No. 41. We will follow that with other possibilities in order to lack of prolongation:

The first case:

When the economic unit achieves profit

Example:

If the value of sales (which is from economic output) = 900$

If the economic evaluation standard = 5

The required:

Economic resultant (the value of net profit)

The value of sales cost (which is from economic inputs)

The solution:

Suppose that the value of the sales cost = C

Economic evaluation standard = (sales value - (C * 0.5)) / (sales value - C)

5 = (900 - (C * 0.5)) / (900 - C)

= (900 - 0.5 C) = (900 - C) * 5

900 - 0.5C = 4500 - 5 C

4.5C = 3600

C = 800

Then Sales cost value = 800$

Economic resultant (profit) = the value of sales – the value of sales cost = 900 – 800 = 100

Two notes:

We came up to the value of the costs itself, which was in the first case of the first possibility in the first conclusion when it was proof (the evaluation standard was equal to 5).

This possibility will be used to set the standard costs of the economic unit when there is a prevalent sale price of the product (in this case, equal to 900 $) and we want to achieve profits at the evaluation standard equal to 5. This possibility will give us the standard cost of the product that we have reached in this case which is equal 800 $

Third possibility of the first conclusion of the theory

If the economic input value and the value of the economic evaluation standard are given to the theory as data (second rib and third rib), the theory will give you the value of the economic outputs (first rib) and the result of the economic system (which is one of the angles of a triangle) as proof.

The following equations are used to extract the value of economic resultant and economic outputs, they are as the following:

The first case:

When the economic unit achieves profit

Example:

If the value of sales cost (which is from economic input) = 800$

If the economic evaluation standard = 5

The required:

Economic resultant (the value of net profit)

The value of sales (which is from economic outputs)

The solution:

Suppose that the value of sales = S

Economic evaluation standard = (S - (value of sales cost * 0.5)) / (S - the value of sales cost)

5 = (S - (800 * 0.5)) / (S - 800)

= (S - 400) = (S - 800) * 5

5S - 4000 = S - 400

4S = 3600

S = 900 =

Value of sales equal 900 $

Economic resultant (profit) = the value of sales - value of sales cost = 900 − 800 = 100

Two notes:

We came up the value of the sales itself, which was in the first case of the first possibility in the first conclusion when it was proof (the evaluation standard was equal to 5).

This possibility is used for the pricing of the product of the economic unit when there is knowledge with the cost value (in our case is equal to 800 $) and we want to achieve profits at the evaluation standard equal to 5, this possibility will give us value of the sale price that we reached (in this case, the sales price will be equal to 900 $)

The second conclusion of the theory

If you give the value of one rib in the previous triangle and the angle which indicates on the result of the work of the economic system, the theory will give you the value of other two ribs (as a proof).

Probabilities of the second conclusion of the theory

First Probability of the second conclusion of the theory and the fourth to the theory

If the value of the economic output (first rib) and the value of the economic result are given to the theory as data, the theory will give you the value of the economic inputs (second rib) and value of economic evaluation standard (third rib) as proof.

The following equations are used to extract the economic input value and the value of the economic evaluation standard, they are as the following:

The first case:

When the economic unit achieves profit

Example:

If the value of sales (which is from economic input) = 900$

If the economic resultant = 100$

The required:

The value of sales cost (which is from economic input).

The economic evaluation standard.

The solution:

Value of sales cost = value of sales - the value of economic resultant = 900 – 100 = 800

Economic evaluation standard = (value of sales - (the value of sales costs * 0.5)) / economic resultant

=(900 - (800 x 0.5)) / 100 = 5

Note: We came up to the value of cost of sales itself, which was in the first case of the first possibility in the first conclusion, which was equal to 800 $. As well as the value of the economic evaluation standard itself when it was equal to 5 when the value of sales is equal to 900 $ and value of economic resultant is equal to 100$

Second Probability of the second conclusion of the theory and the fifth to the theory

If the value of the economic input (second rib) and the value of the economic result (which is one of the angles of a triangle) are given to the theory as data, the theory will give you the value of the economic outputs (first rib) and value of economic evaluation standard (third rib) as proof.

The following equations are used to extract the economic output value and the value of the economic evaluation standard, they are as following:

The first case:

When the economic unit achieves profit

Example:

If the value of sales cost (which is from economic input) = 800$

If the economic resultant = 100$

The required:

The value of sales (which is from economic output).

The economic evaluation standard.

The solution:

The value of the sales = value of sales cost + value of economic resultant
= 800+100=900

Economic evaluation standard= (value of sales - (the value of sales cost * 0.5)) / economic resultant

=(900 - (800 * 0.5)) / 100 = 5

Note: We came up to the value of sales itself, which was in the first case of the first possibility in the first conclusion which was equal to 900 $. As well as the value of the economic evaluation standard when it was equal to 5 when the value of sales cost is equal to 800 $ and value of economic resultant is equal to 100$

Third Probability of the second conclusion of the theory and the sixth to the theory

If the value of the economic evaluation standard (third rib) and the value of the economic result (which is one of the angles of a triangle) are given to the theory as data, the theory will give you the value of the economic outputs (first rib) and value of economic input (second rib) as proof

The following equations are used to extract the economic output value and the value of the economic input, they are as the following:

The first case:

When the economic unit achieves profit

Example:

If the value of economic evaluation standard = 5

If the economic resultant = 100$

The required:

The value of sales (which is from economic output).

The value of sales cost (which is from economic inputs).

The solution:

Value of sales cost = ((economic resultant * evaluation standard) – (Economic resultant)) * 2

((100 * 5) - (100)) * 2 = 800

The value of the sales = value of sales cost + value of economic resultant = 800 +100 = 900

Two notes:

We came up to the value of sales, which equals 900 $ and value of sales cost which equals 800 $, both of them are found in the first case of the first possibility in the first conclusion when the value of economic resultant is 100$ and the economic evaluation standard was equal to 5.

The equations of this possibility are very important because they are used in the preparation of budget (because they determine the value of sales and value of sales cost that should be implemented to achieve the desirable profits at evaluation standard that we identify and aims to profitability) This budget will be used to treat certain diseases that may appear.

Fourthly: Summary of the Probabilities of geometric genetic economy theory:

The first Probability

When the givens are the following

Cost of Sales = 800

Sales Value = 900

The proof will be as following

Activity result value = 100

The degree of economic evaluation standard = 5

The second Probability

When the givens are the following

Sales Value = 900

The degree of economic evaluation standard = 5

The proof will be as following

Activity result value = 100

Cost of Sales = 800

The third Probability

When the givens are the following

Cost of Sales = 800

The degree of economic evaluation standard = 5

The proof will be as following

Activity result value = 100

Sales Value = 900

The fourth Probability

When the givens are the following

Activity result value = 100

Sales Value = 900

The proof will be as following

Cost of Sales = 800

The degree of economic evaluation standard = 5

The fifth Probability

When the givens are the following

Activity result value = 100

Cost of Sales = 800

The proof will be as following

Sales Value = 900

The degree of economic evaluation standard = 5

The sixth Probability

When the givens are the following

Activity result value = 100

The degree of economic evaluation standard = 5

The proof will be as following

Sales Value = 900

Cost of Sales = 800

Note: From the previous above, the geometric infrastructure of the geometric genetic economy theory is valid, and this is due to:

When we provided the data to the theory, the theory enabled us to reach the proof (as a result).

When we used the same proof, the theory enabled us to reach the same previous data.

Notes on the geometric genetic economy theory outputs (indications of economic evaluation standard)

The geometric theory (the theory of genetic economy) achieved the geometric logic, called the economic evaluation standard that is a measuring tool for the work of the economic system (and this is because if the economic evaluation standard mentioned alone, it indicates the success of the economic system or not, this is the basic advantage for using the geometric theory).

Through the use of evaluation standard, we can know the extent of success of the different companies (microeconomic) as well as the various sectors and also the extent of the economic success of the state or not (macroeconomic) generally (see the diagnostic models).

We can also use the evaluation standard in determining the type of disease among the many diseases occurred to either the company or sector or the state. Where the evaluation standard became a diagnostic tool to detect diseases that affect all the cells (genes) which are the component of economic structure, whether for companies or sectors or economic system of the state. The evaluation standard become a diagnostic tool for the genes of these cells, which are the component of the economic infrastructure either for companies, sectors or economic system of the state as we will illustrate in diagnostic models.

Fourth chapter
The use of geometric genetic economy theory in the foundation of economic models
(Practical study of the model of evaluation of companies)

The diagnostic models are divided into:

Diagnostic models at the microeconomic level (companies):

We created several models to detect all the economic problems that face all companies in the world, irrespective of their size, their activities, their nationalities, or the environment which operates in and these models are as the following:

Evaluation model of companies

Aim of the evaluation model of companies:

To know the characteristics of the company as well as to know the economic problems that facing the company and how to treat them.

Inputs of evaluation model for companies:

Value of sales.

Value of sales cost.

Value of general expenses.

Value of the debit interest.

Value of other revenue.

Value of total assets.

A practical example

The following practical example illustrates how to create an evaluation model for the companies and how to discover the economic diseases and how to put treatment spontaneously:

If we had the following data about a company (value of million dollar)

The value of sales (which is from economic output) = 1000$

Value of sales cost (which is from economic input) = 600$

Value of general expenses (which is from economic input) = 350 $

Value of the debit interest (which is from economic input) = 40 $

Value of other revenue (which is from economic output) = 10$

Value of total assets (which is from using of economic sources) = 10000 $

Evaluation process

Firstly: Measure the efficiency of the product of this company

We must know the value of the economic evaluation standard, which measures the efficiency of the product and thus we will recognize that:

Administrative constitution of the company that tells us the volume of production - the elasticity of the products price - to grant discounts on the sale price - to deal with the credit - the company requests from state officials ... etc.)

The characteristics, that should be available in both the production manager, marketing manager, financial manager, and general manager (put the right man in the right place, all that for rationalization of the human element).

Calculation of economic evaluation standard of the product of this company

Calculating gross profit = value of sales - value of sales cost = 1000 - 600 = 400

Calculation of the economic evaluation standard = (value of sales - (value of the sales cost * 0.5)) / gross profit = (1000 - (600 x 0.5)) / 400 = 1.75

Moreover, by reference to output table of the genetic economy theory (indications of economic evaluation standard), we find that value of the standard, which is equal to 1.75 is express an excellent efficient degree of profit and that means:

The administrative constitution of this company

We will mention briefly the main points, as following:

For the volume of the production

It is not required to produce a large number of units in order to cover all expenses to achieve a net profit, which is equivalent to capital, i.e. if the opportunity is given to the company to produce a large number of units, it will have a direct and positive impact on the company's net profit increase .

For elasticity of price of product of this company

This product allows dealing with the discount on the selling price, accommodating the rise in the cost of the product if this happens and can deal with the bank credit.

The characteristics that must be available in each of the production manager, marketing manager, financial manager, and general manager

Firstly: The characteristics that must be available in the production manager

In the case that the degree of economic product efficiency is (Excellent - very good - good) then the characteristics that must be met with the production manager are the following

He must be creative in producing products with high specifications and quality.

Required experience for production is not as important as what is required to improve the quality of the product.

He deals with the production team in a spirit of cooperation.

He does not spare on the product to show the product with specifications and quality required for marketing.

He does not need to work under pressure.

He takes his decision carefully for creativity.

He has more time for creativity.

In the case that the degree of economic product efficiency is (Acceptable - weak - very weak) then the characteristics that must be met with the production manager are the following

He must be able to produce a very large number of the product.

Experience is required for very large Production.

He deals with the production team as a Leader.

He must be very careful about product Costs.

He can cope under a lot of pressure.

He takes his decision quickly to complete what required from him.

He has not a time to achieve the produced quantity.

Secondly: verification of productivity of production management (Production manager)

The production manager must implement the following *budgets*

The basic budget

The credit budgets

The budget for the granting of discounts on the selling price

The budget for increasing the cost of production

The administration must verify the extent of its implementation of previous budgets

Thirdly: relationship of production management with working capital turnover

For the money

Is there the liquidity available to buy raw materials, pay wages and purchase of manufacturing requirements in a timely manner?

Are there available equipment and devices (productive assets) to accomplish what is required of production?

Are there problems in the maintenance of equipment and devices, which lead to a disruption of productivity?

Are there problems in buying a specific quantity of raw materials as well as manufacturing requirements?

Does the company face the problem of the high cost of purchasing the raw materials and manufacturing requirements?

for workers

Are there enough trained employees for production?

Is there clear productive plan for production management?

For the product

Is the company's product produced with the required specifications for marketing (to satisfy consumer desires) which is tested before going out to the market?

Is the cost of the product at the agreed limits with cost department in financial management?

Summary

The result of this model of the genetic economy for management of the production (company name:) summarizes in the following

Firstly: the required features in the production manager (for poor product efficiency)

The production manager is unable to deal under a lot of pressure.

He is slow in making his decision and thus impact negatively on Productivity.

Secondly: Verification of production of production management (production manager)

The productivity of product (A) achieved 80% of the budgets to be achieved in the / / 2

The productivity of product (B) achieved 60% of the budgets to be achieved in the / / 2

The productivity of product (C) 90% of the budgets to be achieved in the / / 2

Thirdly: relationship of production management with working capital turnover

There are problems with liquidity in purchasing raw materials that concern product (B) without availability of hard currency to import them.

There is a problem in the maintenance of productive equipment that concerns product (B) this is due to the absence of a specialist to fix it.

Genetic economy model for the management of marketing

Firstly: The characteristics that must be available in the marketing manager

In the case that the degree of economic product efficiency is (Excellent - very good - good) then the characteristics that must be available in the marketing manager are the following

He can use negotiating style and persuasion in the marketing process.

He has ability to show the quality and specifications of the product.

He has ability to deal with the marketing team with a spirit of cooperation.

He must be creative in dealing with available purchasing power in the market.

He has ability to use the product prices with high flexibility in the marketing process.

He has ability to use the facilities and discounts to promote products of the company.

In the case that the degree of economic product efficiency is (Acceptable – weak - very weak) then the characteristics that must be available in the marketing manager are the following

He can deploy and open new markets.

He has ability to sell a greater amount of product.

He has ability to deal with the marketing team with leader spirit.

He can collect cash.

He can adhere with specific pricing of the products that he markets.

He has ability to adhere to company policies in terms of facilities and discounts.

Secondly: **verification of productivity of marketing management (marketing manager)**

The marketing manager must be able to sell what is mentioned in the following

The basic budget

The credit budgets

The budget for the granting of discounts on the selling price

The budget for increasing the cost of production

The administration must verify the extent of its implementation of previous budgets

Thirdly: **relationship of marketing management with working capital turnover**

For the money
Are there any available funds to make advertising campaigns for the product?
Are there any funds available to deliver the product in the right place for the consumer at the right time?
For workers
Are there enough employees in the marketing department (for sale and collection)?
What is the availability of the qualities required in the marketing team with the requirements of the company's products?
Is the marketing department able to market the excess number of products when the company is dealing with all the credit - discount on the sale price - or increasing the cost of the product?
For the product

What is the duration of the stay of the full product to be sold?

What is the period to collect the value of sales after the sale?

Does the marketing team commit with the company's policies in terms of pricing?

Does the marketing team commit with the company's policies in terms of granting discounts on sales prices?

Does the marketing team commit with the company's policies in terms of granting facilities to customers?

Is there a clear marketing plan for the marketing management?

How does marketing management deal with the purchasing power of the consumer?

The market requirements

Is the marketing gap that is available within a state allowing selling more of this product or requiring opening new markets outside the country?

Does Product fill the desires of the consumer or not? Is the product with specifications and quality required for marketing?

Does the product reach to the consumer at the right time?

Does the product reach to the consumer at the right place?

Did the product define correctly to the consumer?

Does the product reach to the consumer with competition prices?

Is the product able to deal with various consumer purchasing power?

Summary

Here we can write the summary of the genetic economy model for the management of marketing for the company/

Genetic economy model for the financial management

Firstly: The characteristics that must be available in the financial manager

He has logical thinking connecting between the causes and results.

He has patience that enables him to oversee and follow-up.

He must be creative in making the models that give the desired results.

He must bear the responsibility to face the obstacles that occur to the company.

He must be able to communicate with all departments of the company.

Secondly: **verification of productivity or required tasks of financial management (financial manager) which is:**

The follow-up to production management

Does the company have the control system for stocks (wither stores of raw materials or goods ready for sale)?

Does the financial management have a special section for the actual costs and the standard costs for the company's products or not?

Does the company have the necessary liquidity for working capital turnover or not?

Does the financial management have assistant ledger of suppliers in order to know the balances that must be paid?

Does the financial management prepare productive budgets for follow-up in order to verify the production management productivity?

The follow-up to marketing management

Does costs department execute the scientific pricing for the company's products?

Are there follow-up models to know how long the full product takes to be sold?

Are there follow-up models to know how long the marketing department takes for the collection of sales values?

Does the financial management have book in order to analyze the sales to know volume of sales for each product that is sold and the periods when the product is sold?

Does the financial management own the customer assistant ledger to know the balances that desired to be collected?

Is there sufficient liquidity in order to define the company's products?

Is there sufficient liquidity in order to provide the company's products at the right place at the right time?

Does the financial management prepare marketing budgets for follow-up in order to verify the marketing management productivity (marketing manager)?

The follow-up to general expenses

Is there a financial regulation specifies the following?

Who has the expenditure right and adopt aspects of expenditure?

How to determine the review before and after the expenditure.

It determines how to motivate employees and the company's workers.

Is there book for analysis the expenses to control it in order to take the appropriate decision?

Follow-up the loan repayments and the debit interest

Does the financial management advice to deal with banks or prefer to increase their capital?

Does the financial management know the effect of the debit interest on the production and marketing, as well as on the outcome of the income statement?

Does the financial management prepare credit budget in order to cover the debit interest?

Is there an analytic book to repay loans and debit interest?

Follow-up surplus liquidity of the company

Does the financial management exploit the surplus liquidity in the company's activity or outside the company's activity?

What is the effect of achieving other revenue on the company's results?

Follow-up the results of accounting system

Does the financial management check on the movement and balances of the Treasury?

Does the financial management monitor the movement and balances of the bank?

Does the financial management monitor the asset values of the company?

What is the period at which the financial statements are extracted (income statement- the balance sheet - the list of rights of the owners of capital - cash flow statement)?

What are the recommendations of the financial manager as a result of his reading of the financial statements, which improve operational performance of the company?

The company's funds management and insurance of this fund

Does the financial manager do insurance policies on the company's assets as well as their liquidity?

Is there appropriate liquidity in the company for working capital turnover (for purchasing raw material and preparation of the product until it becomes full product to be sold - and then sell the product - then the collection of value of the sales to come back into new working capital turnover)?

Genetic economy model for the general manager

Firstly: The characteristics that must be available in the general manager

In the case that the degree of economic product efficiency is (Excellent - very good - good) then the characteristics that must be available in the general manager are the following

He must have the ability to read the results well in order to take the right decision to correct company's path.

He must be flexible depending on the situation, he shall be strict if necessary and be soft if it is required.

He has the full ability to lead others.

He handles the logic of a father in order to achieve the benefits for employees of the company and at the same time achieving the company's goals.

He has complete ability to communicate and deal with all departments of the company and others.

In the case that the degree of economic product efficiency is (Acceptable - weak - very weak) then the characteristics that must be available in the general manager are the following

He must have the ability to read the results well in order to take the right decision to correct the company's path.

He must be flexible depending on the situation; he shall be strict if necessary and be soft if it is required.

He has the full ability to lead others.

He handles the logic of a father in order to achieve the benefits for employees of the company and at the same time achieving the company's goals.

He has complete ability to communicate and deal with all departments of the company and others.

Other tasks to general manager
(The characteristics of the activity)

In the case that the degree of economic product efficiency is (Excellent - very good - good) then the characteristics that must be available in the general manager are the following

He does not operate under a lot of pressure at work.

He must take decision slowly.

This activity does not require great experience.

He can use financial incentives in order to encourage the workers.

In the case that the degree of economic product efficiency is (Acceptable - weak - very weak) then the characteristics that must be available in the general manager are the following

He operates under a lot of pressure at work.

He must take a decision quickly.

He must have considerable experience that required for activity.

He must be careful in finance spending.

The tasks that should be accomplished by the general manager

In the case that the degree of economic product efficiency is (Excellent - very good - good) then the characteristics that must be available in the general manager are the following

Accreditation of the employment plan in the company, according to the company's needs with specifications that mentioned in genetic economy models for production management, marketing management and financial management.

He must participate with senior management in decision-making about the directed funds to increase investment (fixed assets), these funds can be financed through self-financing or the bank.

He must participate with senior management in decision-making about the directed funds for working capital turnover as these funds can be financed through self-financing or the banks.

He must accredit the budgets for each of:

Budget.

The credit budget, if found.

Budget of discount on the sale price, if found.

Budget of increasing product cost, if found.

He must participate or accredit the company's regulations (financial regulations - the regulations of the company's work).

He must be able to read the actual financial statements in order to know what extent the company has achieved its goals and whether there are obstacles that must be identified and dealt with to be removed in order to achieve the company's goals. The obstacles are summarized as follows:

There is slow in working capital turnover and this is due to one of the following elements:

Shortening in the work of the human element.

There is lack in private cash of working capital turnover.

The product is not with specifications and quality or it has not right price or it is not identified to the consumer in the right place or the right time or the market is saturated from this product.

There is not a good deal with Consumer purchasing power.

Note: It can determine the element that become a reason to slow the working capital turnover by using genetic economy models for each of the production management, marketing management, financial management or the general manager.

There is an extravagance in general expenses and the treatment through the application of financial regulation and good supervision of the aspects of exchange and the review that carried out before and after the exchange, we will know this extravagance through evaluation model.

There is a negative effect from the debit interest on the company's results and the treatment of this effect by replacing the loan through self-financing. This extravagance will be known from evaluation model.

There is excess liquidity in the company that is not exploited in order to achieve other revenue to improve the company's results.

In the case that the degree of economic product efficiency is (Acceptable - weak - very weak) then the characteristics that must be available in the general manager are the following

Accreditation of the employment plan in the company, according to the company's needs with specifications that mentioned in genetic economy models for production management, marketing management and financial management.

He must participate with senior management in decision-making about the directed funds to increase investment (fixed assets), it is preferred to finance solely these funds through self-financing.

He must participate with senior management in decision-making about the directed funds for working capital turnover as it can be financed through self-financing or the banks if marketing manager is able to sell the excess value of sales in order to cover the debit interest

He must accredit the budgets for each of:

Budget.

The credit budget, if found.

Budget of discount on the sale price, if found.

Budget of increasing product cost, if found.

He must participate or accredit the company's regulations (financial regulations - the regulations of the company's work).

He must be able to read the actual financial statements in order to know what extent the company has achieved its goals and whether there are obstacles that must be identified and dealt with to be removed in order to achieve the company's goals. The obstacles are summarized as follows:

There is slow in working capital turnover and this is due to one of the following elements:

Shortening in the work of the human element.

There is lack in private cash of working capital turnover.

The product is not with specifications and quality or it has not right price or it is not identified to the consumer in the right place or the right time or the market is saturated from this product

There is not a good deal with Consumer purchasing power.

Note: It can determine the element that become a reason to slow the working capital turnover by using genetic economy models for each of the production management, marketing management, financial management or the general manager.

There is an extravagance in general expenses and the treatment through the application of financial regulation and good supervision of the aspects of exchange and the review that carried out before and after the exchange, we will know this extravagance through evaluation model.

There is a negative effect from the debit interest on the company's results and the treatment of this effect by replacing the loan through self-financing. This extravagance will be known from evaluation model.

There is excess liquidity in the company that is not exploited to achieve other revenue to improve the company's results.

Secondly: Measuring the efficiency of the company's management for general expenses

We measure the efficiency of the company's management for general expenses to know whether the extravagance happened in these expenses or not. And this by calculating the economic evaluation standard that concerns with these expenses.

Calculation of the economic evaluation standard that concerns with these expenses to this company

Calculating the net profit = value of sales - (the value of the sales cost + value of general expenses)

1000 – (600 + 350) = 50

Calculation of the economic evaluation standard = (value of sales) - ((value of sales cost + value of general expenses) * 0.5) / net profit =

(1000) - (950 * 0.5) / 50 = 10.5

Moreover, by reference to the output table of the theory of genetic economy (indications of economic evaluation standard), we will find that the value of the standard, which is equal to 10.5 is considered acceptable efficiency (for general expenses).

When we compare the standard of product that was equal to 1.75 (Excellent) with standard of general expenses that is equal to 10.5 (acceptable), we will find that the standard of the product has dropped from excellent to acceptable when the company spent the general expenses. In other words, because these expenses have not achieved an excellent efficiency or very good or good, but it achieved acceptable). This indicates the presence of extravagance in this company's general expenses. This illustrates how the model discovers the disease. Therefore, in order to maintain the available economic resources in front of the company, the diagnostic model will come out automatically the budget at the end of the report in order to treat the deficiencies and to maintain those resources.

Thirdly: Measuring the efficiency of the company's management for debit interest

Here we will know whether the company's profits absorbed the debit interest, or the debit interest affected negatively on those profits, by calculating the economic evaluation standard that concerns with debit interest.

Calculation of the economic evaluation standard that concerns with this debit interest to this company

Calculating the net profit = value of sales - (the value of sales cost + value of general expenses + debit interest)

1000 – (600 + 350 + 40) = 10

Calculation of the economic evaluation standard = (value of sales) - ((value of sales cost + value of general expenses + value of debit interest) *0.5) / net profit

(1000) - (990 * 0.5) / 10 = 50.50

Moreover, by reference to the output table of the theory of genetic economy (indications of economic evaluation standard Page No. 32), we will find that the value of the standard, which is equal to 50.5 is considered very poor efficiency (for debit interest).

When we compare the standard of general expenses, which was equal to 10.5 (acceptable) to standard of debit interest, which is equal to 50.5 (very poor), we will find that the standard of general expenses has dropped from acceptable to very poor when the company used the debit interest. This indicates the presence of negative affect from the debit interest on the result of the company, so the diagnostic model will come out the credit budget that should be implemented to determine the value of excess sales to be sold to cover the debit interest in order to treat the deficiencies and to preserve the resources of the company.

Fourthly: Measuring the efficiency of the company's management in achieving other revenue

When the company exploits some of their resources outside its activity in order to achieve other revenues that contribute to improve their results, so we want to know whether these revenues have impacted positively on the company's results or not. Then by calculating the evaluation standard that concerns other revenue as follows:

Calculation of the economic evaluation standard that concerns with other revenue in this company

Calculating the net profit = (value of sales + value of other revenues) - (the value of sales cost + value of general expenses + value of debit interest)

(1000 + 10) – (600 + 350 + 40) = 20

Calculation of the economic evaluation standard = (value of sales+ value of other revenue) - ((value of sales cost + value of general expenses + value of debit interest) * 0.5) / net profit

(1010) - (990 * 0.5) / 20 = 25.75

Moreover, by reference to the output table of the theory of genetic economy (indications of economic evaluation standard), we will find that the value of the standard, which is equal to 25.75 is considered poor efficiency (for other revenue).

When we compare the standard of debit interest, which was equal to 50.5 (very poor) to standard of other revenue, which is equal to 25.75 (poor), we will find that the standard of other revenue has improved from (very poor) to (poor), or we can say that the other revenue has a positive effect on the result of the company.

Fifthly: measuring the efficiency of those responsible for managing the main activity

Here, we can know whether those responsible of the company have managed the working capital turnover in order to achieve profits equivalent to the available economic resources or not. Then by calculating the economic evaluation standard that concerns the efficiency of responsible for managing the main activity as follows:

Calculation of economic evaluation standard of the efficiency of those responsible for the management of the main activity

Calculating the net profit = (value of sales) - (value of sales cost + the value of general expenses)

$(1000) - (600 + 350) = 50$

Calculation of economic evaluation standard = ((value of assets) - (value of assets - net profit) * 0.5) / net profit

$((10000) - (10000 - 50) * 0.5) / 50 = 100.5$

Moreover, by reference to the output table of the theory of genetic economy (indications of economic evaluation standard), we will find that the value of evaluation standard, which is equal to 100.5 is considered poor efficiency (for efficiency of those responsible for the management of the main activity).

Note:

When calculating the efficiency of the responsible for managing the main activity, we have made the standard value from 12, until infinity is the efficiency of the weak in order not to write in the report that efficiency of management is very poor, and this is not recommended .

Moreover, by reference to the value of the standard, which is equal to 100.5 (weak). This indicates the low working capital turnover, and this is due to one of the following four possibilities or all of them. In addition, we can identify any possibility of them by the genetic economy models that concerns production manager, marketing manager, financial manager, and general manager.

Weakness of management efficiency (the human element).

The presence of a physical problem disrupted production (physical element)

The existence of deficiencies in the quality of the product.

The existence of weak purchasing power for consumers.

From the above, and after evaluation of this company, we find the following:

The efficiency of this company's product is excellent.

There is not extravagant in general expenses.

There is the negative impact of the use of debit interest.

There is a positive effect in achieving other revenue.

Efficiency of responsible for the management of this company was poor and this due to weakness of rate of working capital turnover and therefore not achieving profits equivalent to the available economic resources to this company and therefore we must treat the shortening that has occurred in this company through the implementation of the budget. The evaluation model will come out automatically budget in order to achieve profits equivalent to available resources to this company and rationalization for those resources.

Steps of budget preparation

Firstly: the determination of net profit that is equivalent to the available sources to this company

Standard that is equivalent to the available sources is = 4.5 (good degree) this degree is the start point of safety and it is used in an economic recession.

Standard that is equivalent to the available sources is = 3.5 (very good degree) and it is used in the case of the beginning of the economic growth.

Standard that is equivalent to the available sources is = 2.5 (very good degree) and it is used in the case of economic recovery.

So, we will use in the preparation of the budget for this company the equivalent standard that is equal to 4.5 (good degree).

The value of equivalent assets volume = value of assets * equivalent standard = 10000 * 4.5 = 45000

The value of equivalent net assets volume = the value of equivalent assets volume - the value of assets

45000 – 10000 = 35000

Net equivalent standard = equivalent standard - 0.5

4.5 – 0.5 = 4

The value of net assets volume that is not equivalent = (The value of equivalent assets volume / (Net equivalent standard) = 35000 / 4 = 8750

Equivalent net profit = value of assets - The value of net assets volume that is not equivalent

10000 – 8750 = 1250

Secondly: calculating gross profit for this company

Gross profit = equivalent net profit + value of general expenses = 1250 + 350 = 1600

Thirdly: **calculating the value of sales and sales cost that concerns budget for this company**

Using the gross profit which is equal to 1,600 $ and standard of product that has been made previously, which was equal to 1.75 by using one of the possibilities of the geometric genetic economy theory (Third probability of the second conclusion of the theory and the sixth to the theory) to reach the value of sales and cost of sales for the company by the following equations:

Value of sales cost = ((gross profit * standard of product) - (gross profit)) * 2) = (1600 * 1.75) - (1600)) * 2

(2800 - 1600) * 2 = 2400

Value of sales = value of sales cost + gross profit =

2400 + 1600 = 4000

From the above, we can write the budget for this company to treat the shortcomings that happened as follows

The budget

Value of sales	= 4000
(-)The value of sales cost =	2400
Gross profit	= 1600
(-)General expenses value	= 350
Equivalent net profit	= 1250

Very important notes:

Geometric genetic economy theory enabled us to use their equations, which found in their six possibilities in order to discover and determine the disease and work to treat this disease automatically without human intervention, especially when using the programmed model.

From the scientific miracles of the genetic economy that it identified gene of activity of this company (by economic evaluation standard of the product, which was 1.75, which was re-used in the preparation of the budget in order to preserve the genes of this company. If we assume that the activity of this company is the construction activity which is indicated by the evaluation standard 1.75 When we evaluate the budget, we find that the evaluation standard of the product is the same 1.75 as follows

Evaluation standard of the product in budget = ((value of sales) - (value of sales cost) * 0.5) /net profit

(4000 - (2400 x 0.5)) / 1600 =1.75

Thus, the budget will maintain the type of activity of the company. For example, the evaluation standard of product does not equal to 6, which indicates to the activity of the biscuit industry, for example, then the budget will exchange from activity of construction to the activity of the biscuit industry, and this is a big mistake in the preparation of budgets.

Diagnostic model will come out also the credit budget to treat deficiencies as a result of using of debit interest (and with the same steps for preparing the budget, we will prepare the credit budget, so we will mention credit budget without going into mathematical equations that are prepared again for lack of prolongation.

Credit budget

Value of excess sales	= 100
(-)The value of sales cost	= <u>60</u>
Gross profit	= 40

(-)Debit interest = 40

Net profit = zero

Note:

We must work with credit budget in addition to the previous budget.

The beneficiaries from the evaluation model of companies

All companies in the world: apart from their activities, their volume or their legal form and the environment that they operate in it.

Stock exchanges: When any company achieves efficiency of responsible for the management of the main activity and be evaluation standard (excellent - or very good - or good), it means that this company is among the pioneer companies and enter it in the database of the stock market in order to attract investment, especially when company's shares traded on the stock exchange.

Fifth chapter:
Practical study of the model of the preparation of the budget

Aim of the Budget preparation model

Rationalization of the company's available economic resources and exploit them the best use.

Inputs of budget preparation model

The sale price of the unit (product).

The unit cost (product).

Total general expenses (for the year).

Total fixed and current assets.

Practical example

The following practical example illustrates how to prepare the budget preparation model, if we had the following data:

The sale price of the unit = 10$

The unit cost = 8 $

Total general expenses = 250000$

Total fixed and current assets = 1500000$

At targeted efficiency of the budget of (4.5) good degree - the beginning of the safety point.

What is the budget?

The answer:

First, calculate the economic evaluation standard of the product of this company

Calculating gross profit = the sale price of the unit - The unit cost = 10 – 8 = 2

Calculation of the economic evaluation standard = (sale price of the unit – (unit cost * 0.5)) / gross profit

= (10 - (8 x 0.5)) / 2 = 3

Second: determination of net profit that is equivalent to the available sources to this company

By using one of the equations of the theory of geometric genetic economy

The standard that is equivalent to the available sources = (Total assets - (Total assets - equivalent net profit) * 0.5) / equivalent net profit

Assume that the equivalent net profit is = B and the previous equation will be as following:

4.5 = (1,500,000 - (1,500,000 - B) * 0.5) / B

4.5 B = (1500000 - 750000 + 0.5 B)

4 B = 750000

B = 187,500

So, the equivalent net profit is equal to 187,500

Third: **calculating gross profit for this company**

Gross profit = equivalent net profit + the value of general expenses = 187500 + 250000 = 437500

Fourth, **calculating the value of sales and sales cost in the budget for this company**

Using the gross profit, which is equal to 437,500, and evaluation standard of product that has been achieved previously, which was equal to 3. We can use one of the possibilities of theory of geometric genetic economy (Third probability of the second conclusion of the theory and the sixth to the theory) to reach the value of sales and cost of sales for the company by the following equations :

Value of sales cost = ((gross profit * evaluation standard) - (gross profit)) * 2

=((437500 * 3) - (437500)) * 2

(1312500 – 437500) * 2 = 1750000

Value of sales = value of sales cost + gross profit =

1750000 + 437500 = 2187500

From the above, we can prepare the budget for this company as follows

The budget is with good degree

Value of sales	= 2,187,500.00
(-)Value of sales cost	= 1,750,000.00
Gross profit	= 437,500.00
(-)General expenses	= 250,000.00
Equivalent net profit	= 187,500.00

Sixth chapter:
Practical study of the model for the preparation of the standard budget

The aim of the model for preparing the standard estimated budget:

Rationalizing the available economic resources to the company and making the best use of them.

The standard estimated budget provides an opportunity to compare what was done with what was planned in that budget to find out the deviations and their causes and treat those deviations up to date.

Placing everyone in the company with his responsibilities entrusted to it.

The standard budget helps in making decisions regarding reward and punishment based on what has been achieved.

Determine who is responsible for not covering general and administrative expenses in the standard budget.

The standard estimated budget for new projects can be used as a reference in determining the value of general expenses that should not be exceeded to achieve the target of the project.

Inputs to the Budget Preparation model

The selling price of the unit (product)

Unit cost (product)

Total fixed and current assets

Practical example

The following shows how the standard estimate budget model works if we have the following data:

The selling price of the unit (product) = 10 EGP

Unit cost = 8 EGP

Total fixed and current assets = 1,500,000 EGP

When the target budget is efficiently degree as good (4.5) - the start of the safety point

Required: Preparing the standard budge

The answer:

First: Calculating the degree of product efficiency for this company

Calculation of Gross Profit = Selling price of the unit - Unit Cost = 10 - 8 = 2

Calculation of Product Efficiency degree = (Selling price of the unit - (Unit Cost * 0.5)) / Gross Profit

= (10 - (8 * 0.5)) / 2 = 3

Second: Determining the equivalent net profit to the available resources for this company by using one of the equations to geometric genetic economy theory

Estimated Budget Efficiency degree = (Total Assets - (Total Assets - Equivalent Net Profit) * 0.5) / Equivalent Net Profit

Assume that the equivalent net profit = B, and therefore the previous equation is as follows:

4.5 = (1500000 - (1500000 - B) * 0.5) / B

4.5B = (1500000 - 750000 + 0.5B)

4B = 750,000

B = 187500

So equivalent net profit equals 187,500

Third: calculation of sales value of the standard budget

The table that determines the extravagance in general expenses are the following

In case if the economic efficiency degree of the product starts from 1 to 2

The degree of the efficiency standard, which indicates the maximum limits of general expenses that are permitted before the occurrence of extravagance, is degree 4

In case if the economic efficiency degree of the product starts from 2.01 to 4

The degree of the efficiency standard, which indicates the maximum limits of general expenses that are permitted before the occurrence of extravagance, is degree 7

In case if the economic efficiency degree of the product starts from 4.01 to 7

The degree of the efficiency standard, which indicates the maximum limits of general expenses that are permitted before the occurrence of extravagance, is degree 12

In case if the economic efficiency degree of the product starts from 7.01 to 12

The degree of the efficiency standard, which indicates the maximum limits of general expenses that are permitted before the occurrence of extravagance, is degree 50

In case if the economic efficiency degree of the product is greater than 12

The degree of the efficiency standard, which indicates the maximum limits of general expenses that are permitted before the occurrence of extravagance, is degree 1000

Since the Product Efficiency degree in this case is equal to 3 then the standard that indicates to the highest limits of the general expenses and is permissible before extravagance in this case is 7 (see previous table). Based on the above, we will use the standard (which equals 7) and the equivalent net profit (Which is equal to 187500) as data to arrive at the sales cost value at the maximum limit of the standard of non-extravagance in general expenses as follows:

The sales cost value at the maximum limit of the standard of non-extravagance in general expenses = ((equivalent net profit * standard of expense evaluation) - (equivalent net profit)) * 2

= ((187500 * 7) - (187500)) * 2

= (1312500 - 187500) * 2 = 2250000

The sales value of the estimated budget = the sales cost value at the maximum limit of the standard of non-extravagance in general expenses + equivalent net profit

= 2250000 + 187500 = 2437500

Fourth: Calculation of the sales cost value for the standard estimated budget

After we reached to sales value of the standard budget (which is equal to 2437500), which resulted when using the degree of the standard of non-extravagance in general expenses (which was degree 7) based on the above, we will re-use the degree of efficiency of the product of this company (which was equal to 3) in order not to change from the type of activity of this company in order to find the sales cost value for the standard budget, so we will use the sales value (which equals 2437500) and the product efficiency degree of this company (which was equal to 3) as data to arrive at the sales cost value for the standard budget.

Assume sales cost value = S.

Degree of Product Efficiency = (Sales Value - (S * 0.5)) / (Sales Value - S)

3 = (2437500 - (S * 0.5)) / (2437500 – S)

= (2437500 - 0.5S) = (2437500 - S) * 3

= (2437500 – 0.5 S) = 7312500 – 3 S

2.5 S = 4875000

S = 1950000

That is, the sales cost value for the standard estimated budget = 1950000 EGP

Fifth: Calculation of the gross profit of the standard estimated budget

The gross profit of the standard estimated budget = the sales value of estimated budget - the sales cost value of the estimated budget

= 2437500 - 1950000 = 487500

Sixth: Calculation of standard general expenses for this budget

The value of the standard general expenses = gross profit value of the standard estimated budget - equivalent net profit value

= 487500 - 187500 = 300,000

Seventh: From the above, we can prepare the standard estimated budget with a good degree as follows

Sales Value =   2437500

Minus the sales cost value =   1950000

Gross profit =   487500

Minus general expenses =   300000

Equivalent net profit =   187500

Note: The standard budget can be used in the preparation of feasibility studies, especially when it is difficult to determine the general expenses because the project is a new activity that will be practiced with it.

We will confirm from the results achieved

The genetic economy leaves no doubt about the results it extracts, so we find it is confirming the results as follows:

The standard estimated budget took into account the economic situation of the environment in which this company operates, as it used the 4.5 degree for standard which indicates the beginning of the safety point and is used in the case of economic depression. How do we make sure of this? We know this by the degree of efficiency of those responsible for managing the basic activity of the company as follows:

The degree of efficiency of those responsible for managing the basic activity = (Total Assets - (Total Assets - Equivalent Net Profit) * 0.5) / Equivalent Net Profit

= (1500000 - (1500000 - 187500) * 0.5) / 187500 = 4.5 (it is good degree)

It is the same standard that indicates the beginning of the safety point, which is used in the case of an economic depression, as we have applied in our case.

The standard estimated budget maintained the type of activity for this company, as follows:

The efficiency degree of product before preparing the budget was as follows:

Calculation of Gross Profit = the selling price of unit - Unit Cost = 10 - 8 = 2

Calculation of the efficiency degree of product = (The selling price of unit - (Unit Cost * 0.5)) / Gross Profit

= (10 - (8 * 0.5)) / 2 = 3

After preparing the budget, the efficiency degree of product continued as it is 3 degrees in order to preserve the type of activity and it is as follows

Calculation of Gross Profit = Value of Sales - Cost of Sales

= 2437500 - 1950000 = 487500

Calculation of the efficiency degree of product = (Sales value - (Cost of Sales * 0.5)) / Gross profit

= (2437500 - (1950000 * 0.5)) / 487500 = 3

The standard estimate budget has resolved the problem that occurs when the company cannot achieve the estimated budget. How we know the responsible for not covering the general expenses, the marketing manager, or the general manager

If the marketing manager does not achieve the standard sales value (in our case 2437500) then he is considered responsible for not achieving the budget and this is due to his inability to market the standard sales value.

If the achieved general expenses are greater than the standard general expenses (in our case 300,000) then the general manager is considered responsible for the non-implementation of the estimated budget, and this is due to the existence of extravagance in general expenses items. How do we make sure of this? This is what we will know in the following steps:

We make sure of the case of non-extravagance when the general manager achieves general expenses up to an amount of 300,000, at the degree of standard 7, which we used to indicate that there is no extravagance in general expenses

Calculation of Net Profit = Sales value- (Cost of Sales + General Expense)

= 2437500 - (1950000 + 300000) = 187500

General Expense Standard = (Sales Value - (Cost of Sales + General Expenses) * 0.5) / Net Profit

= 2437500 - (1950000 + 300000) * 0.5 / 187500 = 7

It is the standard that indicates the maximum limits of general expenses that are allowed before extravagance occurs, as we have applied in our case this.

The case of extravagance when the general manager achieves general expenses greater than the sum of 300,000, even if one pound

Calculation of Net Profit = Sales value- (Sales cost value + General Expense)

= 2437500 - (1950000 + 300001) = 187499

General Expense Standard = Sales Value - (Sales cost value + General Expense value) * 0.5 / Net Profit

= 2437500 - (1950000 + 300001) * 0.5 / 187499 = 7.000035

It should be noted on the general expense standard that it is transgression 7 degree, which indicates the existence of extravagance in general expenses.

From the above, we find that the standard estimated budget that is extracted by an equation of the genetic economy which has preserved all:

The efficiency degree of preparing the standard budget and consequently on the economic situation (which is 4.5 degrees)

The efficiency degree of the product and thus the activity type of this company (which is 3)

The degree of extravagance standard (which is 7)

This is the scientific miracle of genetic economy, as it was able for the first time to use geometric theory outside of geometric science to reach the highest degree of accuracy in the results.

Seventh chapter:
Practical study of the model of the credit budget preparation

Aim of preparing the credit budget model

Knowledge of the company's ability to deal with bank credit or not.

Bank can know the company's ability to repay the loan through the company's ability to implement each of the budget and credit budget together

Inputs of credit budget preparation model

The sale price of the unit (product)

The unit cost (product)

Total general expenses (for the year)

Total debit interest that will be paid annually

Total fixed and current assets, including the value of the targeted loan

Practical example

The following practical example illustrates how to prepare the credit budget preparation model if we had the following data:

The sale price of the unit = 10 $

The unit cost = 8 $

Total general expenses = 250000 $

Total debit interest that will be paid annually= 50000 $

Total fixed and current assets, including the value of the targeted loan = 1500000 $

At targeted efficiency of the credit budget of (4.5) good degree - the beginning of the safety point

What is the credit budget?

The answer:

In this case, we should prepare the following:

Prepare a budget with good degree

Preparing credit budget to determine the excess sales value that should be sold to cover the debit interest.

Then we must work with both budget and credit budget together as follows:

Prepare Budget with good degree

First: **calculate the economic evaluation standard of the product of this company**

Calculation of gross profit = the sale price of the unit - The unit cost = 10 - 8 = 2

Calculation of the economic evaluation standard = (sale price of the unit - (unit cost * 0.5)) / gross profit

= (10 - (8 * 0.5)) / 2 = 3

Second: **determination of net profit that is equivalent the available sources to this company**

By using one of the equations of the geometric genetic economy theory

The standard that is equivalent to the available sources = (Total assets - (Total assets - equivalent net profit) * 0.5) / equivalent net profit

Assume that the equivalent net profit is = B and the previous equation will be as following:

4.5 = (1,500,000 - (1,500,000 - B) * 0.5) / B

4.5 B = (1500000 - 750000 + 0.5 B)

4B = 750000

B = 187,500

So, the equivalent net profit is equal to 187,500

Third: calculating gross profit for this company

Gross profit = equivalent net profit + the value of general expenses = 187,500 + 250,000 = 437500

Fourth: calculating the value of sales and sales cost of the budget for this company

By using the previous gross profit, which is equal to 437,500 and evaluation standard of product that has been made previously, which was equal to 3. We can use one of the possibilities of geometric genetic economy theory (Third probability of the second conclusion of the theory and the sixth to the theory) to reach the value of sales and cost of sales for the company by the following equations:

Value of sales cost = ((gross profit * evaluation standard) - (gross profit)) * 2

= ((437500 * 3) - (437500)) * 2

= (1312500 - 437500) * 2 = 1750000

Value of sales = value of sales cost + gross profit

= 1750000 + 437500 = 2187500

From the above, we can prepare the budget for this company as follows:

The budget with good degree

Value of sales   = 2,187,500

(-) Value of sales cost   = 1,750,000

Gross profit   = 437,500

(-) General expenses   = 250,000

Equivalent net profit   = 187,500

Credit budget, which sets out the excess sales value that must be sold to cover the debit interest

By using the value of credit cost, which is equal to 50000 (which should be equal to the gross profit of the credit budget as required to cover credit cost (i.e. debit interest) and standard of product that has been achieved previously, which was equal to 3. We can use one of the possibilities the theory of geometric genetic economy to reach the value of sales and value of sales cost for the company by the following equations:

Value of sales cost = ((gross profit * evaluation standard) - (gross profit)) * 2

= ((50000 * 3) - (50000)) * 2

= (150000 - 50000) * 2 = 200000

Value of sales = value of sales cost + gross profit =

= 200,000 + 50,000 = 250000

From the above credit budget can be written for this company as follows:

Value of excess sales	= 250,000
(-) Value of sales cost	= 200,000
Gross profit	= 50,000
(-) Debit interest	= 50,000
Net profit	= 0.00

We must work with budget and credit budget together as follows

Sales value of the budget = 2,187,500

The value of excess sales to cover the debit interest = 250,000

The value of total annual sales that are required to be sold = 2,437,500

In the case that the marketing manager is able to market the value of total annual sales, then the company is dealing with this credit, in the case of the inability of the marketing manager to sell the value of total annual sales, then the company refrains with dealing in this credit.

Beneficiaries from the credit budget preparation model:

All companies that are likely to deal with bank credit.

All banks that lend companies.

Eighth chapter:
Practical study of the model of the preparation of the budget when the cost of the product rises

The aim of preparing of the budget model when the value of sales cost increases

We will know the extent of the product flexibility to absorb the increased costs in order to stay competitive in the market without the company has to raise prices.

Inputs of the budget preparation model when the value of sales cost increases

The sale price of the unit (product).

The unit cost (product) before the cost increases.

The unit cost (product) after the cost increases.

Total general expenses (for the year).

Total fixed and current assets.

Practical example

The following practical example illustrates how to prepare the budget model when the value of sales cost increases if we had the following data:

The sale price of the unit = 10 $

The unit cost (product) before the cost increases = 8 $

The unit cost (product) after the cost increases = 9 $

Total general expenses = 250000 $

Total fixed and current assets = 1500000 $

At targeted efficiency of the credit budget of good degree - the beginning of the safety point.

What is the budget model when the value of sales cost increases?

Answer:

In this case, we must prepare the following:

Prepare a budget with a good degree before the cost increases.

Prepare a budget with a good degree after the cost increases.

Then we find out the value of excess sales that required to be sold in order to achieve the same profit that achieved before the cost increases.

Preparation of budget with good degree before the cost increases

First: **Calculation of the economic evaluation standard of the product of this company**

Calculating gross profit = the sale price of the unit - The unit cost = 10 - 8 = 2

Calculation of the economic evaluation standard = (sale price of the unit - (unit cost * 0.5)) / gross profit

= (10 - (8 * 0.5)) / 2 = 3

Second: **determination of net profit that is equivalent the available sources to this company**

By using one of the equations of the theory of geometric genetic economy

The standard that is equivalent to the available sources = (Total assets - (Total assets - equivalent net profit) * 0.5) / equivalent net profit

Assume that the equivalent net profit is = B and the previous equation will be as following:

4.5 = (1,500,000 - (1,500,000 - B) * 0.5) / B

4.5 B = (1500000 - 750000 + 0.5 B)

4B = 750000

B = 187,500

So, the equivalent net profit is equal to 187,500

Third: **calculating gross profit for this company**

Gross profit = equivalent net profit + the value of general expenses = 187,500 + 250,000 = 437500

Fourth: **calculating the value of sales and sales cost of the budget for this company**

By using the gross profit which is equal to 437,500 and evaluation standard of product that has been achieved previously, which was equal to 3. We can use one of the possibilities of theory of geometric genetic economy (Third probability of the second conclusion of the theory and the sixth to the theory) to reach the value of sales and cost of sales for the company by the following equations:

Value of sales cost = ((gross profit * evaluation standard) - (gross profit)) * 2

= ((437500 * 3) - (437500)) * 2

= (1312500 - 437500) * 2 = 1750000

Value of sales = value of sales cost + gross profit =

1750000 + 437500 = 2187500

From the above, we can prepare the budget for this company as follows:

The budget with good degree is

Value of sales	= 2,187,500
(-) Value of sales cost	= 1,750,000
Gross profit	= 437,500
(-) General expenses	= 250,000
Equivalent net profit	= 187,500

Preparation of budget with good degree after the cost increases

First: calculate the economic evaluation standard of the product of this company

Calculating gross profit = the sale price of the unit - The unit cost after the increase

= 10 - 9 = 1

Calculation of the economic evaluation standard = (sale price of the unit - (unit cost * 0.5)) / gross profit

= (10 - (9 * 0.5)) / 1 = 5.5

Second: determination of net profit that is equivalent to the available sources to this company

By using one of the equations of the theory of geometric genetic economy

The standard that is equivalent to the available sources = (Total assets - (Total assets - equivalent net profit) x 0.5) / equivalent net profit

Assume that the equivalent net profit is = B

so, the previous equation will be as following:

4.5 = (1,500,000 - (1,500,000 - B) * 0.5) / B

4.5 B = (1500000 - 750000 + 0.5 B)

4B = 750000

B = 187,500

So, the equivalent net profit is equal to 187,500

Third: calculating gross profit for this company

Gross profit = equivalent net profit + the value of general expenses = 187,500 +250,000 = 437500

Fourth, calculating the value of sales and sales cost of the budget for this company

By using the gross profit which is equal to 437,500 and evaluation standard of product that has been achieved previously, which was equal to 5.5. We can use one of the possibilities of theory of geometric genetic economy (Third probability of the second conclusion of the theory and the sixth to the theory) to reach the value of sales and cost of sales for the company by the following equations:

Value of sales cost = ((gross profit * evaluation standard) - (gross profit)) * 2

= ((437500 *5.5) - (437500)) * 2

= (2406250 - 437500) * 2 = 3937500

Value of sales = value of sales cost + gross profit =

= 3937500 + 437500 = 4375000

From the above we, can prepare the budget for this company as follows:

The budget with a good degree after cost increases is

Value of sales   = 4375000

(-) Value of sales cost   = 3937500

Gross profit   = 437500

(-) General expenses   = 250000

Equivalent net profit   =187500

The increase in the value of sales due to increase the cost of sales

The value of sales after the increase = 4375000

(-) The value of sales before the increase = 2187500

The increase in the value of sales as a result of increased cost = 2187500

In case that marketing manager is able to sell the value of excess sales because of increased cost, so the administration will accredit this increase or increase sales price.

Beneficiaries of the budget preparation model when the value of sales cost increases

All companies in the world, especially industrial companies.

Ninth chapter:
Practical study of the model of the preparation of the budget when we grant discounts on the selling price

Aim of preparation of budget for granting discounts on the sale price of the product

We will know the extent of the product flexibility to absorb the value of a discount in order to stay competitive in the market without having to regression of granting of these discounts.

Inputs of Preparation of budget for granting discounts on the sale price of the product:

The sale price of the unit (product) before discount.

The sale price of the unit (product) after discount.

The unit cost (product).

Total general expenses (for the year).

Total fixed and current assets.

Practical example

The following practical example illustrates how to prepare the budget model when we grant the discount on the sale price of the product if we had the following data:

The sale price of the unit before discount = 10 $

The sale price of the unit after discount = 9 $

The unit cost (product) = 8 $

Total general expenses = 250000 $

Total fixed and current assets = 1500000 $

At targeted efficiency of budget for granting discounts on the sale price of the product with (4.5) good degree - the beginning of the safety point.

What is the budget model when we grant the discount on product sale price?

Answer:

In this case, the following must be prepared:

Prepare a budget with a good degree before granting the discount.

Prepare a budget with a good degree after granting the discount.

Then we find out the value of excess sales that required to be sold in order to achieve the same profit that achieved before granting the discount.

Preparation of budget with a good degree before granting the discount:

First, calculate the economic evaluation standard of the product of this company

Calculating gross profit = the sale price of the unit - The unit cost = 10 - 8 = 2

Calculation of the economic evaluation standard = (sale price of the unit - (unit cost * 0.5)) / gross profit

= (10 - (8 * 0.5)) / 2 = 3

Second: determination of net profit that is equivalent to the available sources to this company

By using one of the equations of the theory of geometric genetic economy

The standard that is equivalent to the available sources = (Total assets - (Total assets - equivalent net profit) * 0.5) / equivalent net profit

Assume that the equivalent net profit is = B

And the previous equation will be as following:

4.5 = (1,500,000 - (1,500,000 - B) * 0.5) / B

4.5 B = (1500000 - 750000 + 0.5 B)

4B = 750000

B = 187,500

So, the equivalent net profit is equal to 187,500

Third: **calculating gross profit for this company**

Gross profit = equivalent net profit + the value of general expenses = 187,500 + 250,000 = 437500

Fourth: **calculating the value of sales and sales cost of the budget for this company**

By using the gross profit which is equal to 437,500 and evaluation standard of product that has been achieved previously, which was equal to 3. We can use one of the possibilities of theory of geometric genetic economy (Third probability of the second conclusion of the theory and the sixth to the theory) to reach the value of sales and cost of sales for the company by the following equations:

Value of sales cost = ((gross profit * evaluation standard) - (gross profit)) * 2

= ((437500 * 3) - (437500)) * 2

= (1312500 - 437500) * 2 = 1750000

Value of sales = value of sales cost + gross profit =

=1750000 + 437500 = 2187500

From the above, we can prepare the budget for this company as follows:

The budget with good degree

Value of sales = 2,187,500

(-) Value of sales cost = 1,750,000

Gross profit = 437,500

(-) General expenses = 250,000

Equivalent net profit = 187,500

Preparation of budget with a good degree after granting the discount

First, calculate the economic evaluation standard of the product of this company

Calculating gross profit = the sale price of the unit - The unit cost

= 9 - 8 = 1

Calculation of the economic evaluation standard = (sale price of the unit - (unit cost * 0.5)) / gross profit

= (9 - (8 * 0.5)) / 1 = 5

Second: determination of net profit that is equivalent to the available sources to this company

By using one of the equations of the theory of geometric genetic economy

The standard that is equivalent to the available sources = (Total assets - (Total assets - equivalent net profit) * 0.5) / equivalent net profit

Assume that the equivalent net profit is = B

and the previous equation will be as following:

$4.5 = (1,500,000 - (1,500,000 - B) * 0.5) / B$

$4.5 \, B = (1500000 - 750000 + 0.5 \, B)$

$4B = 750000$

$B = 187,500$

So, the equivalent net profit is equal to 187,500

Third: calculating gross profit for this company

Gross profit = equivalent net profit + the value of general expenses

= 187,500 + 250,000 = 437500

Fourth: calculating the value of sales and sales cost of the budget for this company

By using the gross profit which is equal to 437,500 and evaluation standard of product that has been achieved previously, which was equal to 5. We can use one of the possibilities of theory of geometric genetic economy (Third probability of the second conclusion of the theory and the sixth to the theory) to reach the value of sales and cost of sales for the company by the following equations:

Value of sales cost = ((gross profit * evaluation standard) - (gross profit)) * 2

= ((437500 * 5) - (437500)) * 2

= (2187500 - 437500) * 2 = 3500000

Value of sales = value of sales cost + gross profit =

= 3500000 + 437500 = 3937500

From the above, we can prepare the budget for this company as follows:

The budget with a good degree after granting the discount

Value of sales = 3937500

(-) Value of sales cost = 3500000

Gross profit = 437500

(-) General expenses = 250000

Equivalent net profit = 187500

The increase in the value of sales due to grant the discount

The value of sales after granting the discount = 3937500

(-) The value of sales before granting the discount = 2187500

The increase in the value of sales because of granting the discount = 1750000

In the case, that marketing manager is able to sell the value of excess sales because of granting the discount, and then the administration will accredit this discount or rethink about this discount.

Beneficiaries of the budget preparation model when we grant the discount on the sale price

All companies in the world

Tenth chapter:
The use of geometric genetic economy theory in the foundation of Economic Models of Macroeconomics (Practical study of the model of diagnosis of the sectors of the State)

Evaluation Model of the sectors of the state (macroeconomic):

Aim of the evaluation model of sectors of the state:

Knowledge of the economic problems that faces each sector of the sectors of the state and how to treat them through using the tools of financial, monetary and legislative policy.

Inputs of evaluation model of sectors of the state:

Total economic inputs that are required for the sector evaluation.

Total economic outputs that are required for the sector evaluation.

Total expenses that are used by the sector that required to be evaluated.

Total cost of credit facilities that are provided by financial companies in this sector that required to be evaluated.

Total available economic resources (Total fixed assets, total current assets and investment assets) that are required for this sector evaluation.

Practical example:

If you had the following data for the agriculture sector (Value in Billions):

Value of sales (the value of economic outputs for this sector) = 30 $

Value of sales cost (the value of the economic sector inputs) = 15 $

Value of expenses (to complete the working capital turnover, this is from economic inputs of the sector) = 3 $

Value of debit Interest that is used in this sector (this is from economic inputs of the sector) = 3 $

Value of other revenues that is achieved by this sector (this is from economic outputs of the sector) = 3 $

Value of available investment to this sector = 30 $

Operation of sector evaluation

The aim of sector evaluation

Sector evaluation aims to provide the tools that lead to the success of the companies, where these tools do not insert in the scope of the work of the managements of these companies. The state owns these tools to correct the course of the work of these companies in order to achieve self-sufficiency from goods and services - the elimination of unemployment - increasing purchasing power for workers in this sector - increasing of state revenues and these tools are:

Financial policy (most important are customs duties and support of production inputs - taxes ...etc).

Monetary policy (most important is the debit interest rate - the exchange rate ... etc).

Laws and conventions (most important are investment attraction laws - international conventions and laws to stimulate the market - ban of importation of similar goods).

First: measure the efficiency of the products of this sector

We must know the value of the economic evaluation standard, which measures the efficiency of the products of this sector and therefore we can know how to use financial policy where if:

Efficiency standard of sector products is (excellent - very good - good) as the standard value starts from 1 to 7, it means that the products of this sector achieve big gross profit, making it able to withstand all the productive burdens (such as customs duties and other productive fees, it means that this sector does not need to support).

Efficiency standard of sector products is (acceptable - poor - very poor - Loss), any standard will start from 1 to 7, it means that the products of this sector achieve poor gross profit, making this sector needs to reduce productivity burdens or the state gives the support to this sector if it presents strategic products for the citizens.

Calculation of economic evaluation standard of the products of this sector

Calculating gross profit of the sector = Total value of sector sales - Total value of sector sales cost

= 30-15 = 15

Calculation of economic evaluation standard = (value of sales - (the value of sales cost * 0.5)) / gross profit

= (30 - (15 * 0.5)) / 15 = 1.5

By reference to output table of geometric genetic economy theory (indications of evaluation standard), we find that the standard value which is equal to 1.5 is considered excellent efficiency, it means that the sector is able to withstand all the productive burdens which are used through the financial policy (such as customs duties and other productive fees).

Second: **calculation of efficiency of sector management for general expenses:**

Calculating the sector's net profit = Total sales of the sector - Total sales cost of sector + general expenses of this sector) = 30 - (15 +3) = 12

Calculation of evaluation standard = (Total sales of the sector - (Total sales cost of sector + general expenses of this sector) * 0.5)) / net profit

= (30 - (15 + 3) * 0.5) / 12 = 1.75 (is excellent efficiency)

Third: measuring the efficiency of management of the sector for the debit interest

We must know the value of the economic evaluation standard, which measures the management efficiency of the sector in the debit interest in order to see whether the bank credit affects negatively on this sector or not:

If the sector has not been affected negatively from debit interest. The state will follow the monetary policy that should be implemented in the country in terms of the stability of the debit interest rate.

If the sector has been affected negatively from the debit interest it has become imperative for officials to follow the monetary policy to keep pace with this sector, where they can reduce the debit interest rate.

Calculating the sector's net profit = Total sales of the sector - Total sales cost of sector + general expenses of this sector + debit interest of the sector)

= 30 - (15 +3 + 3) = 9

Calculation of evaluation standard = (Total sales of the sector - (Total sales cost of sector + general expenses of this sector + debit interest) * 0.5)) / net profit

= (30 - (15 + 3 +3) *0.5) / 9 = 2.16 (very good efficiency)

When we compare the standard of sector management efficiency for the debit interest that is equal to 2.16 (very good) to standard of sector efficiency for general expenses that is equal to 1.75 (excellent). We find that this sector has been affected by the value of the debit interest where the standard of general expenses falls from 1.75 (excellent) to 2.16 (very good) for debit interest. However, it is noted that the debit interest standard still achieves high efficiency (very good). It indicates that this sector is still able to bear burden debit interest and can deal with the credit and thus it is not required from officials to reduce interest rates.

Fourth: measurement of responsible efficiency for the management of this sector including bank credit

Knowing the value of the economic evaluation standard, which measures the total efficiency of the officials in all operating companies in this sector for the management of the main activity, including the bank credit aims to know their ability to rotate the working capital and achieve equivalent profit to available economic resources, as we know the following:

If the value of the efficiency standard of those responsible for the management of this sector, including bank credit is (excellent - very good - good) that indicates that this sector:

An attractive sector for investment (because it achieves big equivalent profit from the available economic resources).
This sector does not need marketing (because it has succeeded to run working capital).
Officials can impose the progressive tax (or additional tax) in the case of lack of commitment of the operating companies in this sector to reduce prices in order to adjust the market and increase the purchasing power in the case if the state needs this procedure.

If the value of the standard of efficiency of those responsible for the management of this sector, including bank credit is (acceptable - poor - losses) that indicates that this sector:
This sector needs help in marketing (as those responsible for this sector require holding international conventions for the revitalization and marketing of products of the sector or stop similar goods).
The companies that produce the strategic products to the state can be given support.

Calculation of the sector's net profit = Total sales of the sector − (Total sales cost of sector + general expenses of this sector + debit interest of the sector)

= 30 − (15 + 3 + 3) = 9

Calculation of evaluation standard = (value of assets − (the value of assets − net profit) * 0.5) / net profit

= (30 − (30 − 9) * 0.5) / 9 = 2.16 (very good efficiency)

(The efficiency standard equal to 2.16 is (very good), so this standard can be used as an ID for companies and sectors to indicate its efficiency).

From above, we know that this sector is attractive for investment and it does not require marketing and holding international conventions to activate the products of this sector. The responsible can also impose a progressive tax (or additional tax) in the case of lack of commitment of operating companies in this sector to reduce prices in order to adjust the market and increase purchasing power.

Beneficiaries of the evaluation model of state sectors

Registered companies in this sector.

All the ministers and those responsible for managing the various sectors in the country (the agricultural sector - industrial - commercial - service ... etc.)

Eleventh chapter:
Practical study of the model of diagnosis of the economic system of the state

Evaluation model of the economic system as a whole

Aim of Evaluation model of the economic system as a whole

Here, we will know the extent of improvement in the purchasing power of members of the society and thus the achievement of social justice.

Inputs of evaluation model of all sectors of the state

Total economic output for all operating companies in the state (sales).

Total economic input for all operating companies in the country (cost of sales).

Total expenses that have been used by all operating companies in the country (general expenses).

Total cost of the credit facilities that is used by operating companies in the country (debit interest).

Total available economic resources (Total fixed assets, total current assets and investment that are available to all operating companies in the country).

Example:

If we had the following data about a country (value in Billions):

Value of sales (the value of economic output) = 30$

Value of sales cost (the value of the economic input) = 15$

Value of expenses (to complete the working capital turnover) (one of the economic inputs) = 3$

Value of debit interest (one of the economic inputs) = 3$

Value of other revenue (one of the economic outputs) = 3$

Value of Investments that are available to all operating companies in the country = 30$

The process of evaluating of the economic system

Evaluation of the state aims to know whether the state does its role toward to its citizens or not.

Where the most important roles of the state in economic terms are summed up in the following:

Increase the volume of investment while maintaining the success of the existing investments in the country in order to:
Self-sufficiency of goods and services with the increase in the volume of these goods and services in order to reduce their prices to be suitable for purchasing power of the community members.
The elimination of unemployment and poverty because of the opening of new investment projects.
Achieving appropriate profits to shareholders in these projects.
Increasing the sovereign revenue of the state, as well as the volume of the additional revenue by:
Optimal use of natural resources in the state without waste.
Achieving sovereign revenues resulting from taxes and fees.
Encourage scientific innovations in the state to achieve appropriate returns from these innovations.
Achieving additional revenues through investment in pioneer companies which their efficiency is (excellent - very good - good).
Sovereign revenues as well as additional revenues are used to achieve the following:

Achieving food, treatment, housing, education and cheap means of transport in order to support these requirements from revenues of state, especially for the laboring classes in the country.

Below we will know the evaluation of the state through the degree of efficiency of the management of State resources where we will know through this efficiency the most important indicator; this indicator is available purchasing power in that state. Purchasing power is resulting from the volume of the investment and what government spends to support the needs of the citizens. This stops on two basic conditions:

The first condition:

There is a law in this country determines the minimum wage and salaries, whether in the public or private sector (very important), where this law works to balance between the purchasing power and commodity prices and services in the state, or the exploitative will appear in society and the capitalists will exploit the working class in this state.

The second condition:

Economic system management efficiency must concern special products that are sold in the local market (without use of the purchasing power of the other countries, which is through export so as to determine the extent of the contribution of the local purchasing power of the community members in order to manage working capital that concern the operating companies in the country).

Evaluation of the economic system of this state as following

Calculation of net profit = Total sales value - (the value of the total cost of sales + value of general expenses + value of debit interest) = 30 - (15 + 3 + 3) = 9

Calculation of evaluation standard = (value of asset - (value of assets - net profit) * 0.5) / net profit

= (30 - (30 - 9) * 0.5) / 9 = 2.16 (very good)

What does that mean?

This standard indicates that the state managed the working capital that concerns all operating companies in the country, resulting in the volume of products (whether goods or services), these products have found a buyer (after excluding products that have been exported abroad, and dealt with other purchasing power than local). In this case, the efficiency degree of the state is very good, and this indicates that the purchasing power and traded on the economic system of this country is great. With essential condition that unless there is a law that sets minimum wage and salaries in order to meet the basic needs of employees and workers, the economic evaluation of this state will be meaningless.

The question here is, if the economic system of a country achieved poor efficiency degree, what does responsible disposal toward the economic system management (the Prime Minister)?

The answer to this question, the official must take several decisions as following:

If this state is rich, it should support the goods and services or to increase the purchasing power of its citizens by increasing wages and salaries or give cash grants to them.

If this state is poor, there is a defect in the entry of individuals. The state must impose a progressive tax (or additional tax) on companies that raise their prices without justification in order to increase the purchasing power of the community members.

Twelfth chapter:
The use of geometric genetic economy theory in the foundation of economic models Third: The economic model of the global economy (Practical study of the diagnostic model of companies that are registered on the stock exchange)

The aim of the diagnostic model of companies listed on the stock exchange

In dealing with multinational companies (the axis of the global economy), most of these companies are listed on the international stock exchanges. Therefore, they must know the basics to be considered when investing in such companies.

This model designed to decrease the losses that speculators, investors in that deal in shares in various stock exchanges incurred.

Where all of the investors or speculators before dealing in the stock shares using either financial analysis or technical analysis has to recognize the answer of the following three questions in order to avoid losses.

First question:

Is the company that you want to buy its shares about to liquidation or not?

Where the law defines in most countries of the world if the company losses half its capital value, the law makes compulsory liquidation.

The question is: Do you buy shares of the company on the verge of liquidation like someone who bought a house about to collapse?

Second question:

What is the number of recovery years of shares?

The number of recovery years is defined as the number of years in which the book value per shares reaches the market value of the share, assume that the company achieved earning equivalent to the value of the alternative opportunity. (Safe limits to the number of recovery years are two years).

The question is: would you accept to deal in the shares of the company with a very large number of recovery years like who make a deal and fall down from the sky and does not know to what abyss will settle?

Third question:

What is the efficiency of the company owning the shares?

The efficiency of the company determines the ability of the company to achieve profits and thus the distribution of coupons on the shares where the distribution of coupons for shares, supports the operation of buying and selling not only in the case of investment, but also in the case of speculative where the speculator does not have to sell his shares in the case of falling prices, but compensates it by receiving coupons until stock prices improve (and efficiency of companies is divided into: excellent – very good – good – acceptable – poor –losses).

The question is: Do you prefer when you interacted with the shares to be supported by the company efficiency or be forced to realize losses when prices fall down?

This model will answer the previous three questions when you purchase any shares in the stock market in order to reduce your losses.

Input of the diagnostic model of companies listed on the stock exchange as follows:

Nominal value.

Total shareholding equity = (capital + reserves + profits – loss if found).

Number of shares.

Market value.

Sales value.

Purchase's value.

General expenses value.

Debit interest value.

Other revenue value.

Total asset value.

Practical example:

If we had the following data about a company listed on the stock exchange (value of million dollars):

Nominal value = 10 $

Total shareholding equity = (capital + reserves + profits – loss if found) =

(5000000 $ + 150000 $ + 350000 $) = 5500000 $

Number of shares = 500000 shares

Market value = 12 $

Sales value = 30 $ (value of million dollar)

Purchase's value = 15 $ (value of million dollar)

General expenses = 3 $ (value of million dollar)

Debit interest = 3 $ (value of million dollar)

Other revenues = 3 $ (value of million dollar)

Total assets = 30 $ (value of million dollar)

The answer:

Answer to the first question:

Is the company that you want to buy its shares about to liquidation or not?

First:

Calculate the book value of this company = total shareholding equity /number of shares

= 5500000 / 500000 = 11 $

Second:

Percentage of increasing of book value and its comparing to nominal value per share = (Book value / nominal value) * 100 % = (11 / 10) * 100 % = 110 %

If the ratio of book value was equal or less than 50% from the nominal value, we do not recommend dealing in the shares of this company because the company has lost a lot of its capital and required liquidation.

If the ratio of book value was greater than 50% and less than 100% of nominal value, then caution is required when dealing on the shares of this company because it lost part of its capital.

If the ratio of book value was greater than 100% of nominal value, this encourages investment, especially if the answers to the second and third question are as positive as in our company.

Answer to the second question:

What is the number of recovery years of shares?

First:

Calculating the value of the risk amount = Market value - Book value = 12 - 11 = 1 $

Second:

Calculate earnings per share = Book Value * annual interest of the bank (In our case is 8%)

= 11 * 8% = 0.88 $

Third:

Calculating the number of recovery years = The value of the of risk amount / earnings per share

= 1 / 0.88 = 1.1363 years (It is less than 2 years that are allowed)

In the case of this company, the number of recovery years within two years (in the safe border) and therefore this share encourages to buy, especially if the answer to the first and the third question is positive.

The answer of the third question:

What is the efficiency of the company owning the shares?

Calculation of net profit of the company= (Total value of sales of the company) − (value of the total cost of sales of the company + value of general expenses of this company + value of debit interest of the company)

= 30 - (15 + 3 + 3) = 9

Calculation of Evaluation Standard = (Value of Assets − (Value of Assets − Net Profit) * 0.5) / Net Profit

= (30 - (30-9) * 0.5) / 9 = 2.16

(This company has achieved very good efficiency)

For investors, the efficiency of the company preferably is (excellent − very good − good) to get coupons better than the returns of banks.

For speculators, it is not wise to choose shares that achieved an efficiency of loss, but he has the freedom to choose in the top competencies.

Purchase decision or not:

Since this company has achieved profits, where the nominal value was equal to 10 $ which became 11 $ as book value, these profits increased the shareholding equity by 10%, indicating that this company should not be liquidated.

This company achieved a number of recovery years are two years (within the safe border).

This Company has achieved very good efficiency.

From the above, we find that the answer to the previous three questions is positive, which encourages the decision to buy the shares of this company.

Comparing between economic systems:

First: Ownership of the components of production

In the genetic economy

Ownership of the elements of production is privately and subjected to the law of supply and demand with public ownership in limits 10% of the pioneer companies (the pioneer companies are companies that achieve profits more than the banks' profits).

In the capitalist economy

Private ownership subjected to the law of supply and demand only

In the socialist economy

Public ownership, their values are determined by the state.

Second: Management of production elements

In the genetic economy

Subjected to who have private property

In the capitalist economy

Subjected to who have private property

In the socialist economy

Management of production elements is subject to the state

Third: Self-sufficiency

In the genetic economy

Self-sufficiency is achieved when the state achieves goals of the private ownership and through the employment of both human capital and physical capital directly by using the financial and monetary policy tool

In the capitalist economy

It can be achieved only in the presence of an abundance of natural resources resultant and the resulting output of the technological innovations of the state

In the socialist economy

It cannot be achieved because of waste of natural resources and weakness of technological innovations

Fourth: Trade freedom

In the genetic economy

It can achieve that easily because of the presence of economic database

In the capitalist economy

Most countries try to achieve trade freedom through the application and implementation of international conventions

In the socialist economy

It does not depend on trade freedom

Fifth: Ownership of output of the production elements

In the genetic economy

The private sector has outputs (revenue) of the production elements with the state is owning of part of this revenue within the limits of its ownership of the elements of production by 10%

In the capitalist economy

The private sector has full output (revenue) of production elements

In the socialist economy

The State has full output (revenue) of production elements

Sixth: Microeconomic structure

In the genetic economy

This economy depends mainly on joint-stock companies to attract investment directly with different values

In the capitalist economy

This economy is based on the different types of companies (Shareholding Companies- recommendation- solidarity-individuals...etc.)

In the socialist economy

This economy is based on state-owned enterprises (public sector- governmental sector

Seventh: Cycle of Savings and investment

In the genetic economy

Attracting savings through the use financial and monetary policy tools and employ them directly without the moderator, leading to:

Absorbing of unemployment

The presence of added value as a result of actual production

Increasing purchasing power for many segments of society

In the capitalist economy

Attracting savings through a moderator (financial institutions such as banks) and then re-employ this savings, causing the following:

Increasing of unemployed funds and focusing its at few categories

Investment trends towards profitable sectors than others

Weakness of purchasing power to many classes of society that is leading to troubling, poverty and sometimes unemployment

In the socialist economy

The state does the financial employment (investment) because the state has the elements of production, but the value of the elements of the production will be weak with time for the following reasons

The volume of expenditure is more than revenues due to mismanagement

The existence of unproductive disguised unemployment

Wasting of natural resources and weakness of technological innovation outputs

Eighth: State revenues and expenditure

for example, infrastructure, and social Justice (Education - Health - Subsidies ... etc.)

In the genetic economy

Volume of state revenues stops in the volume of each of:

Resultant of state ownership of the elements of production (10 percent) and this revenue is huge, and burden doesn't fall on the micro economy which increases the volume of state revenues

The outputs of financial and monetary policy tools in the management of micro-economics (as taxes - Customs - fees, etc.) and this revenue is burdened on the microeconomic units and the state can alleviate this burden according to the revenue earned from pioneer companies the (10 percent)

Outputs of natural resources and outputs of technological innovations

As a result of achieving all these revenues, it enables the state to achieve its objectives (strong state - an advanced, infrastructure - providing subsidies - health services - educational services ... etc)

In the capitalist economy

Volume of state revenues stops on the volume of each of:

The outputs of financial and monetary policy tools in the management of micro-economy (as taxes - Customs - fees, etc.) and this revenue is burdened on the microeconomic units

Outputs of natural resources and outputs of technological innovations

Through the volume of the public revenues of the state, it enables the state to achieve its objectives (strong state - an advanced, infrastructure - providing subsidies - health services - educational services ... etc.)

In the socialist economy

We mentioned that the state has the outputs (revenues) and the burden of expenses falls on the state too, and for mismanagement, the country has become debt and thus the required services will be less

Ninth: Evaluation of economic system

In the genetic economy

Evaluation at the microeconomic level

Genetic economy has models capable of diagnosing and treating any economic unit as follows:

It identifies genes of products and the degree of risk

It identifies genes of workers and their compatibility with the genes of the products

It determines if the gene of product allows dealing with credit or not

It determines the efficiency of the economic unit (whether they are from pioneer companies or stumbled companies

It determines the reasons of troubling (in human capital, physical capital, or factors outside the economic unit transactions) and treats the causes of troubling.

Evaluation at the macroeconomic level

We mentioned that the diagnosis and treatment model of the state sectors is able to divide the companies and thus the sectors as following

Troubled sectors for reasons outside the control of economic units and the state is working on the treatment in order to maintain the human capital and physical capital by using of financial and monetary policy tools

Pioneer sectors that benefit in the following:

Making database that determines pioneer companies in order to attract capital (whether local or global)

Database helps the companies to achieve the trade freedom between companies.

Database of the pioneer companies (withers local or global) enables the state to

invest in pioneer companies (10%) to achieve profits to face public expenditure

We note that the genetic economy is capable of diagnosis and treatment in order to provide sound economic system without any failure

In the capitalist economy

Evaluation at the microeconomic level

This economy has analytic tools and comes on top of these analytic tools is financial analysis. It uses several equations that specialists are only able to interpret these equations where their views differ according to their expertise

Evaluation at the macroeconomic level

Macroeconomic evaluation depends on some indicators as the following: -

Unemployment rate

The investment rates

Inflation

public debit

Balance of Payments

We note that these indicators do not provide treatment to be followed, but the treatment depends on who has experience in this economy

In the socialist economy

Evaluation at the microeconomic level

Evaluation tools are non-existent at the macroeconomic level. We measure the extent of the unit's ability to achieve the budget that prepared by the state

Evaluation at the macroeconomic level

We evaluate the macroeconomic through the state's ability to carry out the tasks entrusted to them Example:

Ability to employ the human capital (even if there is disguised unemployment)

Ability to employ physical capital (even if it led to the achievement of losses due to mismanagement)

Volume of products (even if it did not satisfy the desires of consumers)

Volume of providing services (regardless of its quality)

We note that the socialist economic system did not have the tools for evaluation to detect diseases, but it relied on its ability to implement the plan without looking at how the disease arises and its causes and thus the treatment of these diseases

Questions and exercises at the genetic economy

What is the definition of the genetic economy?

Define all of the (microeconomics - macroeconomics - the global economy), as defined by the genetic economy?

Mention diseases that infect (microeconomics - macroeconomics - the global economy).

Mention the seven genes that used by genetic economy and their characteristics?

How is the employment and investment in the curriculum of the genetic economy?

How does genetic economy achieve revenue without, the citizens or companies bear the burden?

What are the goals that achieved from model of evaluation and diagnosis of companies?

What are the objectives that achieved from the budget preparation model?

What are the objectives that achieved from the standard budget preparation model?

What are the objectives that achieved from credit budget preparation model?

What are the objectives that achieved from preparation model of the budget when the cost of the product increases?

What are the objectives that achieved from preparation model of the budget when granting discounts on the sale price?

What are the objectives that achieved from evaluation and diagnosis model for sectors of the state?

What are the objectives that achieved from evaluation and diagnosis model for the economic system?

If you are a member of the Human Resources Committee to employ a production manager and this data is available to you as the following:

Cost of Product Unit is 400 $ and the sale price of the product unit is 1000 $ and annual general expenses are 100000 $ and total assets are 1,000,000 $

Two persons have come to fill this job and their characteristics were as following:

First Person

He cares with specifications and product quality.

He cares with development of product and spending on this development.

He prefers to deal with the production team in a spirit of cooperation.

He prefers to take his decision carefully and does not work under pressure in order to reach a good product.

Second Person

He cares about the desired production volume.

He is very careful about product costs.

He prefers to deal with a production team as a leader.

He prefers to take a decision quickly and firmly and works under the pressure in order to accomplish what is required.

The question is which person you will choose to fill this job at this company and why?

If you are a member of the Human Resources Committee to employ marketing manager and this data is available to you as the following:

Cost of product unit is 0.25 $ and the sale price of the product unit is 0.35 $ and annual general expenses are 100000 $ and total assets are 1,000,000 $

Two persons have come to fill this job and their characteristics were as following:

First Person

He has ability to use negotiation and persuasion in the marketing process.

He has the ability to highlight the quality and specifications of the product.

He prefers to deal with the marketing team with a spirit of cooperation.

He is creative in dealing with the purchasing power of consumers

He prefers to use the credit facilities in the sale

Second Person

He has ability to deploy and open new markets to market the company's products.

He has ability to sell a greater amount of production.

He prefers to deal with the marketing team as a leader.

He has an ability to cash collection.

He is committed with specific prices and policies of the company

The question is which person you will choose to fill this job at this company and why?

What are the characteristics needed in financial manager as defined by the genetic economy?

What are the tasks that will be performed by the financial manager as defined by genetic economy?

What are the characteristics needed in general manager as defined by the genetic economy?

What are the tasks that will be performed by the general manager as defined by genetic economy?

If you have the following data:

Cost of product unit is 400 $ and the sale price of the product unit is 1000 $ and annual general expenses are 100 000 $ and total assets are 1,000,000 $

There is a trend that the company will borrow an amount of 250,000 $ with annual interest rate of 25000 $

If you knew that the company is able to sell 500 units of this product every year

The question: does this company execute this loan or not?

If you have the following data:

Annual sales value is 500 000 $ and the value of the annual cost of sales 350 000 $ and value of annual general expenses is 140 000 $ and total assets 1,000,000 $

The question: Does the extravagance in the general expenses happens in this company or not? If it happened, how do you identify the causes? And how you treat this wasteful?

If you have the following data:

Annual sales value is 500 000 $ and the value of the annual cost of sales 350 000 $ and value of annual general expenses is 50000 $ and total assets 250000 $

If the market value of the shares of this company is equal to the book value

The question: Do you recommend buying shares of that company or not? Please mention the causes that led you to take this decision in order to invest in this company (not speculation).

If you have the following data:

If the prevailing price in the market for this product is 10 $ and the cost of the product is 15 $ and the value of annual general expenses is 140 000 $ and total assets 1,000,000 $

The question: what do you recommend the management of this company and why?

If you have the following data for a new project of its kind:

Value of cost of product Unit is 8 $ and sale price of product unit value is 10 $ and values of total assets are 1,500,000 $

The question: How do you determine the value of the standard general expenses (the maximum of expenses) for this project?

If you have the following data:

If the value of unit cost of the product before the increasing is 8 $ and value of unit cost of the product after the increasing is 9 $ and the sale price of the product unit is 10 $ and the value of the annual general expenses is 140 000 $ and total assets is 1,000,000 $

If you knew that this company is able to sell 200,000 units annually

The question: Does this company have to raise the selling price to compensate the increased cost of the product, or the selling price and volume of annual sales will absorb this increase?

If you have the following data:

Cost of Product Unit is 8 $ and the sale price of the product unit is 10 $ and the value of the annual general expenses is 140 000 $ and total assets is 1,000,000 $

If you knew that the company's management would like to give discounts on the sale price of 10%

Also, if you knew that this company is able to sell 300,000 units annually

The question: Can this company accredit this discount or regress this decision?

If you've got the following data for one sector (Value in Billions)

Annual sales value is 30 $ and the value of the cost of sales is 15 $ and total investments (assets) in this sector is 30 $

If you knew that responsible for the management of this sector want to impose an additional tax to adjust the price in this sector

The question: What do you recommend this responsible and what are the reasons that you depend on?

If you've got the following data for one sector (Value in Billions)

Annual sales value is 50 $ and the value of the cost of sales is 30 $ and values of general expenses is 15 $ and total investments (assets) in this sector are 100 $

If you knew that responsible for the management of this sector want to stop importing similar products which produced by this sector

The question: what do you recommend this responsible and what are the reasons that you depend on?

What are the conditions to be met before the evaluation of the economic system of any country?

If you have the following data for a company listed on the Stock Exchange and its data as follows:

Nominal value per share = 10 $

Total shareholding equity = (5 million dollars as capital +150,000 $ as reserves +350000 $ as profits) Total = 5500000 $

Number of shares = 500,000 shares

Market value per share = 12 $

The value of the company's revenues or the value of the sales for a whole year = 30 $ (value in billion dollars)

Value of the cost of revenue or the value of purchases for a full year = 15 $ (value in billion dollars)

Gross profit = Value of sales - Value of purchase = 15 $ (value in billion dollars)

The value of general expenses, including depreciation for a full year = 3 $ (value in billion dollars)

The value of debit interest for a full year = 3 $ (value in billion dollars)

Value of external revenues for the whole year = 3 $ (Value in billion dollars)

Net profit = (15 $ gross profit) - (3$) general expenses + 3$ debit interest) = 9 $ billion dollars

Value of total fixed and current assets = 30 $ (value in billions of dollars)

If you are consulted, is it possible to invest in this company or not, what is your answer? And why?

References

D / Mohammed Ahmed Sorour - Production Management - Ain Shams Library - 44 El Qasr al-Aini - Cairo 1983 -

D / Mohammed Hamed Timraz - Specialized Accounting - Ain Shams Library - 44 El Qasr al-Aini - Cairo 1985 -

D / Abdel Moneim Ahmed Tuhami - Finance - Introduction to facilities and financial markets - Ain Shams Library - 44   El Qasr al-Aini - Cairo 1983 -

D / Mohamed Abd El-Aziz Abdul-Karim - financial management and financial planning - Dar Arab renaissance - 32 Street Abdel Khalek Tharwat – Cairo

D / Zainab Seif al-Nasr - production management - library Trade and Cooperation - 30 Sri Ismail enlightening Street   Cairo 1988

D / Hassan Mohamed Kamal - Management Accounting - Ain Shams Library - 44 El Qasr al-Aini –Cairo

D / Mr Nile Festival - the new labor law - Dar Arab renaissance - 32 Abdel Khalek Tharwat Street – Cairo

Kamal Abdul Hamid Necati - studies in corporate accounting - Ain Shams Library - 44 El Qasr al-Aini -   Cairo 1984 -

D / Ali Mohammed sweet - lectures on procurement management - Ain Shams Library - 44 El Qasr al-Aini - Cairo 1983 -

 D / Ahmed Mohamed Moussa - performance analytical study assessing critical view indicators 1983 -

Shawqi Mahmoud Atallah - government and national accounting - Youth Library - 26 Sri Ismail u Mounarh -   Cairo

D / Fathi happy holiday - the scientific principles for the accounting of actual costs - Ain Shams Library - 44 El Palace Aini - Cairo 1984 -

D / Mohammed Ahmed Sorour - Operations Research in Management - Ain Shams Library - 44 El Qasr al-Aini - Cairo 1984 –

Mohammed Sabri Al Attar - cop entrance in Management Accounting – Journal of Social Sciences -University Kuwait 1985 - - Issue 2 - Volume 13, from page 83 to page 103

Ali Mahmoud Abdul-Rahim - behavioral aspects of planning budgets – Journal of Social Sciences – University Kuwait 1985 - - Issue 1 - Volume 13, from page 91 to page 120

Mr. Morsi incumbent ElDesoki - accounting development general budget of the services sector using the concept of analysis systems - Journal of Social Sciences - Kuwait University - 1988 page 183 to page 211

D / Hamdiya Zahran - economic development - Ain Shams Library - 44 El Qasr al-Aini - Cairo 1982 -

D / Abdul Qader my dream - the tax on commercial and industrial profits –Arab Renaissance Publishing House - 32 Abdel Street Khalek Tharwat - Cairo 1983

D / Abdul Aziz Mari - d / Abdo Ibrahim Issa - the money and the banks - First Edition - Press Commission statement 27 Arab mosque Ismaili -- 1,962

D / Hamdi Ahmad Anani - the economics of public finance under the Private Enterprise Systems - appointed library Sun - 44 El Qasr al-Aini - Cairo 1985 -

D / Hatem Sami Afifi - Foreign trade theory - Ain Shams Library - 44 El Qasr al-Aini – Cair 1982- 1983

D / Hamdi al-Anani - Public Financial Economics (theories and policies) – Ain Shams Library - 44 El Qasr al-Aini - Cairo 1982 -

D / Mohamed el-Sayed Said - transnational corporations and the future of the national phenomenon - the world of knowledge - Kuwait -1986

Boualem Ben Gilani - Fred Bashir Tahir - Towards a theory of the Muslim consumer behavior – Journal of Social Sciences - Kuwait in 1989 - from page 43 to page 67

Fathi Khalil El Khadraoui - the relationship between excess domestic liquidity and balance of payments deficit in developing countries Non-oil 1968 - 1983 - Journal of Social Sciences - Kuwait - 1987 p. 39 to p. 74

D / glorious Massoud - Planning economic and social progress - the world of knowledge - Kuwait 1984

D / Abdul Khaleq Abdullah - the contemporary world and international conflicts - the world of knowledge - Kuwait 1989 -

Mahdi Ismail Alhzan - international experiences in privatization - lessons from the experiences of Malaysia, New Zealand Mexico - Journal of Social Sciences - Kuwait - 1996 from page 129 to page 159

Abdul Rahman Abdul Baqi Omar - Studies in the Behavioral Sciences - Ain Shams Library - 44 El Palace   Aini - Cairo

D / Abdullah Aweys - Math economy - Ain Shams Library - 44 El Qasr al-Aini - Cairo -   1982

D / Najla while Mortagi - personnel management - Ain Shams Library - 44 El Qasr al-Aini - Cairo - 1985

Hassan Mohamed Khairuddin - Introduction Behavioral Sciences - Dar-generation printable - 14 Pearl Palace - Faggala

D / Mohammed Jalal Abu-Dahab - Applied Statistics - - Ain Shams Library – 44 El Qasr al-Aini – Cairo

D / Mohammed Jalal Abu-Dahab - analytical statistical - Ain Shams Library – 44 El Qasr al-Aini – Cairo

Artis. M.J (1984): << Macroeconomics >>, Oxford university press.
Dornbusch. and Fischer.S (1990): << Macroeconomics >>, Sixth edition, international Edition, New York.
Fisher. S (1992): << Does macroeconomic policy matter? Evidence from developing countries >>, ICEG, Calfomis.
Michner. R (1998): << Inflation expectation and out - put: Lucas Island Revisited >>. Journal of macroeconomics, vol No 4.
Sergent. T (1997), << Relation expectations and inflation >>, Harper and Row, New York.
Taylor, J (1979): << Staggered wages in a Macro- Model >>, The American Economic Review, and proceedings, May.

www.ingramcontent.com/pod-product-compliance
Lightning Source LLC
Chambersburg PA
CBHW050000230526
45465CB00003BB/1198